DEDICATION

This book has been written for and is dedicated to those traders and investors who believe the financial markets are influenced by more than valuation multiples, analyst models and academic portfolio theories.

CONTENTS

M.G. Bucholtz

FIGURES

TABLES

ACKNOWLEDGMENTS

To my beautiful wife Jeanne, without whose help and support none of my books would have been possible.

DISCLAIMER

Recommended Readings

The Universal Clock, J. Long, (P.A.S. Publishing, USA, 1993)

McWhirter Theory of Stock Market Forecasting, L. McWhirter, (Astro Book Company, USA, 1938).

Stock Market Forecasting – The McWhirter Method De-Mystified, M.G. Bucholtz, (Wood Dragon Books, Canada, 2014)

The Universe Within, N. Turok, (House of Anansi Press, Canada, 2012)

A Theory of Continuous Planet Interaction, Tony Waterfall, (NCGR Research Journal, Volume 4, Spring 2014, pp. 67-87).

Gann for the Active Trader, Daniel Ferrera, (Wasendorf & Associates Inc, USA, 2006).

New Concepts in Technical Trading Systems, J. Welles Wilder, (Hunter Publishing Company, USA, 1978)

1

INTRODUCTION

Many market analysts and financial media commentators think daily news, quarterly earnings reports and corporate events drive stock prices.

I disagree.

Call me a rebel, call me a radical, call me what you may. I have never been one to resign myself to mainstream thinking. I believe there is something else that drives the financial markets.

In 2002, when I decided to become an Investment Advisor, I joined a small investment firm in western Canada that had a reputation for thinking outside the box. I was mentored by two seasoned Investment Advisors who deepened my understanding of technical chart analysis. I learned that markets shift from being in an uptrend to being in a downtrend and back again across both short and longer time horizons. I learned that if I followed these trend changes using technical chart analysis I would be in tune with the rhythm of the markets. This refreshing approach represented a clear break from the academic financial theory espoused as part of the exam regimen required for the licensing process with the Investment Dealers Association of Canada. And thus began my quest to delve into the uncanny and esoteric forces that align with trend changes in the financial markets.

In 2003, after a series of reflective discussions with a fellow Investment Advisor, I applied to join a local Masonic Lodge. Early on in my Masonic education, I was urged to contemplate the hidden mysteries of science and nature through further study of the harmony between arithmetic, geometry and astronomy. Nature comprises the whole of our material universe from the solar system all the way to the smallest measurable particle of matter. Science is the disciplined use of mathematics to describe our material universe in terms of prediction and control. The process of contemplating the mysteries of science and nature is what Masons call enlightenment.

As I delved further into the relationship between science and nature, I learned the venerable market trader, W.D. Gann, had been a Mason as well. Gann spent much of his trading career pursuing enlightenment through the study of sacred math and astrological phenomena and applying it to his trading of stocks and commodity futures. Knowing that Gann had been a Mason piqued my curiosity and my journey to learn more about the forces that affect the financial markets took on an almost urgent tone. I began to devour literature related not only to the ideas of W.D. Gann but also to esoteric mathematical patterns of science and nature.

My journey reached a fortuitous turning point many years later, in May 2012, when I attended the United Astrology Conference in New Orleans, USA. I quickly learned I was not alone on my journey. There were many others like me on a similar quest to understand the forces that drive the financial markets. I was so enthused by this Conference that I decided to do something I had never before done – write a book.

In March 2013, I released *The Bull, the Bear and the Planets – Trading the Financial Markets Using Astrology*. But, like so many first time authors, my enthusiasm resulted in me not providing enough examples and not explaining the concepts clearly enough. So much so, that many readers seeking knowledge of basic financial astrology were unsure of how to properly apply the astrological concepts presented in the book. I have since gone on to publish several other books on the subject of financial astrology, but the shortcomings of *The Bull, the Bear and the Planets* have been haunting me. As 2016 dawned, I decided the time to do a re-write into an easier-to-read, easier-to-use format had arrived.

So, if daily news, quarterly earnings reports and corporate events do not drive the markets, then what does?

I am of the opinion that the financial markets are a reflection of the mass psychological emotion of traders, investors and fund managers. When market participants are feeling positive, they are driven to buy. When they are feeling uncertain or negative, they are driven to sell.

Probing this idea deeper immediately yields the complex question - what fuels human emotion?

Medical researchers still have not definitively answered this question. Some say changes in blood alkalinity or acidity define our emotions. Some say changes in chemical hormones in the bloodstream are at the root of our emotions. My humble opinion on this complex matter is that human emotion is electromagnetic. I believe the ever-changing configuration of orbiting planets and other celestial bodies in our cosmos electromagnetically influences our body chemistry and our emotions.

This opinion has been shaped by the many Astrology publications I have read over the past several years including Tony Waterfall's insightful article from the *Spring 2014 NCGR Research Journal*. In his article, Waterfall reminds readers that the Sun is the centre of our planetary system. The Sun emits massive amounts of solar radiation in all directions into the vastness of space. This radiation is called *solar wind*. This solar wind interacts with the magnetic fields around Mercury, Venus, Moon, Mars, Jupiter, Saturn, Uranus, Neptune and Pluto. These planets accept and then disburse the solar wind radiation. As the radiation is disbursed, a significant amount of it finds its way towards the magnetic field around planet Earth. Changes in the density and speed of solar wind mean that the amount of radiation reaching Earth's magnetic field on a daily, weekly or monthly basis will be ever-changing. As a result, the intensity, or flux, of the Earth's magnetic field is also constantly changing. The alignment of the orbiting planets in our cosmos also plays a role in determining how much solar radiation is deflected towards Earth's magnetic field.

A simplistic way of viewing this entire arrangement is to think of a billiards table as the cosmos. The various balls on the table are the planets and other celestial bodies. The solar radiation is the white cue ball bouncing and deflecting off other balls on the table. The human body is largely comprised of water which is a conductor of electricity. We all have an electrical field that runs through our tissues. Hence, basic physics demands that changes to the Earth's magnetic field will then induce subtle changes to our bodily electrical circuitry. These subtle changes, in my opinion, are what drive our emotional responses.

There is so much more to be understood. Scientists and psychologists who are on a quest to learn more have come to call the developing science of how the cosmos affects humans *cosmo-biology*.

Ancient civilizations as far back as the Babylonians recognized cosmo-biology, but in a more rudimentary form. Their high priests tracked and recorded changes in the emotions of the people. These diviners and seers tracked events, both fortuitous and disastrous. Although they lacked the ability to comprehend the physics of solar wind and magnetic fields, they were able to visually spot planets Mercury, Venus, Mars, Jupiter and Saturn in the heavens. They correlated changes in human emotion and societal events to these planets. They assigned to these planets the names of the various Deities revered by the people. They further identified and named various star constellations in the heavens and further divided the heavens into twelve signs. This was the birth of astrology as we know it today.

Starting in the early 1900s, esoteric thinkers such as Wall Street trader W.D. Gann noted that basic astrology bore a striking correlation to changes on the financial markets. This was the birth of financial astrology. Gann based his writings and forecasts on the synodic cycles between various planets. Gann also delved deep into esoteric math, notably square root math. He is well remembered for Gann Lines – a technique based on square roots.

But Gann lived in a challenging time. Statute laws in places such as New York expressly forbade the use of occult science (which astrology was considered to be) in business ventures. Gann therefore carefully concealed the basis for his market forecasts. Today many traders and investors try to emulate Gann but they do so in a linear fashion. What they are missing is the astrology component, which is anything but linear.

In the 1930s, Louise McWhirter followed closely in Gann's footsteps. She identified an 18.6 year cyclical correlation between the general state of the American economy and the position of the North Node of the Moon. Her predictive methodology included noting the dates when the Moon passed by key points of the natal birth horoscope of the New York Stock Exchange. As well, she identified a correlation between price movement of a stock and those times when transiting Sun, Mars, Jupiter and Saturn each made hard aspects to the natal Sun position in a stock's natal birth horoscope.

The late 1940s saw a further advancement in the field of financial astrology when astrologer Garth Allen (a.k.a. Donald Bradley) produced his *Siderograph Model*. This complex model is based on aspects between the various transiting planets. Each aspect as it occurs is given a sinusoidal weighting as the *orb* between the planets varies. This model is as powerful today as it was in the late 1940s.

As you read these words, I invite you to think about the collapse in Oil prices which started in June 2014 at a Mercury Retrograde event just as the transiting Sun passed exactly by the natal position of the North Node in the 1983 natal birth horoscope wheel of Crude Oil futures.

I further invite you to think back to August 2015 and the market selloff that apparently nobody saw coming. The reality is that this selloff started at a confluence of three events. August 2015 marked an Inferior Conjunction of heliocentric Venus to Earth, a Venus Retrograde event and the appearance of Venus as a Morning Star after having been only visible as an Evening Star for the past 263 days.

I further invite you to think about the market weakness that marked the onset of calendar year 2016. This volatility came at the ¾ point of the larger Saturn-Jupiter cycle, the cycle that W.D. Gann called the 'Master Cycle'. This weakness also marked the mid-way point between August 2015 and June 2016 when Venus will be at Superior Conjunction and will appear as an Evening Star again. This weakness also came at a Mercury Retrograde event.

The commonality between these few examples of market behavior is cyclical time. But not the type of time we read off our watches, calendars and digital displays on our laptop computers. The markets are driven by the cyclical movements of planets in orbit around the Sun. As I was crafting this manuscript, I began searching for an analogy that best described the movement of markets in the context of orbiting planets. The title *Cosmic Clock* is what emerged.

When applying astrology to trading and investing, it is vital at all times to be aware of the price trend. There are many ways of quantifying trend. My personal experience has shown me that the chart indicators developed by J. Welles Wilder are very effective. In particular, his DMI and his Volatility Stop are two indicators that should be taken seriously. As a trader and investor, what you are looking for is a change of price trend that aligns to an astrology event. When you see the trend change, you should take action.

Whether that action means implementing a long position, a short position or just tightening up on a stop loss will depend on your personal appetite for risk and on your investment and trading objectives. Astrology is not about trying to take action at each and every astrology event that comes along. Not all astrology events are powerful enough to induce a change of trend. Such is the mystery of the cosmos.

I sincerely hope after you have applied the material in this book to your trading and investing activity, you will embrace financial astrology as a valuable tool to assist you in decision making.

Observing the heavens in relation to events on Earth is nothing new. Consider the words of these leading thinkers on this phenomenon:

"An unfailing experience of mundane events in harmony with the changes occurring in the heavens, has instructed and compelled my unwilling belief." (Johannes Kepler – astronomer, mathematician 1571-1630)

"Heaven sends down its good and evil symbols and wise men act accordingly." (Confucius – Chinese philosopher 551-479 BC)

"The controls of life are structured as forms and nuclear arrangements, in relation with the motions of the universe." (Louis Pasteur-scientist 1822-1895)

"Oh the wonderful knowledge to be found in the stars. Even the smallest things are written there...if you had but skill to read." (Ben Franklin-one of the Founding Fathers of America 1706-1790)

"It's common knowledge that a large percentage of Wall Street brokers use Astrology." (Donald Reagan, formerly Ronald Reagan's Chief of Staff)

M.G. Bucholtz

2

BASIC ASTROLOGY & THE ZODIAC

Astrology is an ancient science focused on the correlation between the planets, events of nature and behaviour of mankind. This ancient science is rooted in thousands of years of observation across many civilizations.

- The ancient Sumerians, Akkadians and Babylonians between the 4th and 2nd centuries BC believed the affairs of mankind could be gauged by watching the motions of certain stars and planets. They recorded their predictions and future indications of prosperity and calamity on clay tablets. These early recordings form the foundation of modern day astrology.

- Ancient Egyptian artifacts show that high priests Petosiris and Necepso who lived during the reign of Ramses II were revered for their knowledge of astrology. The Egyptian culture is thought to have developed a 12 month x 30 day time keeping method based on the repeated appearances of constellations.

- Ancient Indian and Chinese artifacts reveal that astrology held an esteemed place in those societies for many thousands of years.

- Hipparchus, Pythagoras and Plato are key names from the Greek era. Historians think Pythagoras assigned mathematical values to the relations between celestial bodies. Plato is thought to have offered up predictions relating celestial bodies to human fates. Hipparchus is thought to have compiled a star catalogue which popularized astrology.

- In the latter years of the Roman empire, astrology was used for political gain. Important military figures surrounded themselves with philosophers such as Ptolemy and Valens. In 126 AD, Ptolemy penned four books describing the influence of the stars. His works are collectively called the *Tetrabiblos*. In 160 AD, Valens penned *Anthologies* in which he further summarized the principles of astrology.

Following the conversion of Emperor Constantine to Christianity in 312 AD, using astrology for gain became a crime according to the Church of Rome. Astrology then began a slow retreat to the sidelines where for the most part it remains today. Despite astrology's repression by a Church seeking to protect its authority, the science was still used by leading thinkers such as Galileo, Brahe, Nostradamus, Kepler, Bacon and Newton. Thanks to the tenacity of these men, astrology was prevented from fading away altogether into a distant memory.

The Zodiac

The Sun is at the center of our solar system. Earth, Moon, Mercury, Venus, Mars, Jupiter, Saturn, Uranus, Neptune and Pluto and various other asteroid bodies complete our planetary system. The various planets and other asteroid bodies rotate 360 degrees around the Sun following a path called the *ecliptic plane* as shown in Figure 1. Earth is slightly tilted (approximately 23 degrees) relative to the ecliptic plane. Projecting the Earth's equator into space produces the *celestial equator plane*. There are two points of intersection between the ecliptic plane and celestial equator plane. These points are commonly called the *vernal equinox* (occurring at March 20th) and the *autumnal equinox (occurring at September 20th)*.

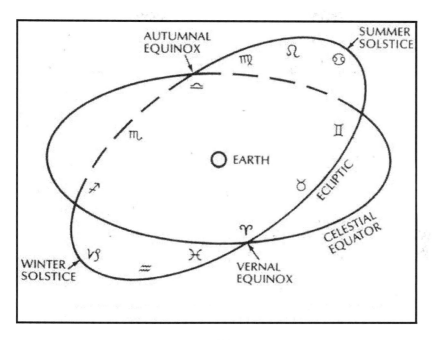

Figure 1 The Ecliptic

Dividing the ecliptic plane into twelve equal sections of 30 degrees results in what astrologers call the *zodiac*. The twelve portions of the zodiac have names including Aries, Cancer, Leo and so on. If these names sound familiar, they should. You routinely see all twelve names in the daily horoscope section of your morning newspaper. Figure 2 illustrates a *zodiac wheel*. The starting point or zero degree point of the zodiac wheel is the sign Aries. From our vantage point here on Earth, the Sun is located at zero degrees Aries at the vernal equinox (March 20th) of each year.

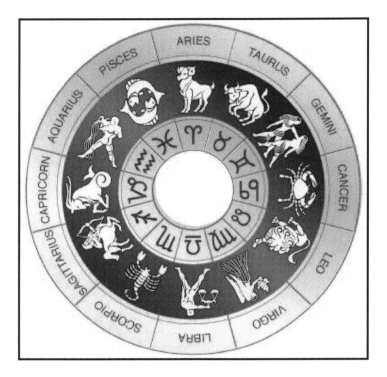

Figure 2 The Zodiac Wheel

Geocentric and Heliocentric Astrology

Astrology comes in two distinct varieties – *geocentric* and *heliocentric*. In *geocentric* astrology, the Earth is taken to be the vantage point for observing the planets as they pass through the signs of the zodiac. Owing to the different times for the various planets to each orbit the Sun, from an astrologer's vantage point on Earth, it appears as though from time to time certain planets make distinct angles (called *aspects*) with one another and also with the Sun. The *aspects* that are commonly used in astrology are 0, 30, 45, 60, 90, 120, 150 and 180 degrees. In financial astrology, this list is simplified. As you will learn in this book, aspects of 0, 90, 120 and 180 degrees are the most commonly used ones in financial astrology.

In *heliocentric* astrology, the Sun is taken to be the vantage point and to an observer positioned on the Sun, it likewise appears as though various planets are making angles with other planets from time to time.

Most of the examples you will see throughout this book are based on *geocentric* astrology, but I will show how *heliocentric* astrology plays a role in timing the markets as well.

Ascendant, Descendant, MC and IC

As the Earth rotates on its axis once in every 24 hours, an observer situated on Earth will detect an apparent motion of the zodiac. Astrologers further apply four cardinal points to the zodiac, almost like the north, south, east and west points on a compass. The east point is termed the *Ascendant* and is often abbreviated Asc. The west point is termed the *Descendant* and is often abbreviated Dsc. The south point is termed the *Mid-Heaven* (from the Latin *Medium Coeli*) and is often abbreviated MC. The north point is termed the *Imum Coeli* (Latin for bottom of the sky) and is abbreviated IC.

These cardinal points are often used when applying astrology to the markets. For example, when the New York Stock Exchange officially opened for business on May 17, 1792, it had its Ascendant in Cancer, its MC in Aries, its Descendant in Capricorn and its IC in Libra.

If you have ever wondered about the names of the zodiac wheel portions, the following descriptions may be of interest. To ancient civilizations, each of these twelve signs was named after groupings and patterns of stars visible in the heavens to the high priests.

The Signs

Aries (The Ram)

(0 to 30 degrees) 21 March – 20 April

According to Greek mythology, Nephele, the mother of Phrixus and Helle, gave her sons a ram with a golden fleece. To escape their evil stepmother, Hera, the sons mounted the ram and fled. When they reached the sea, Helles fell into the water and perished. Phrixus survived the ordeal and upon arriving in Colchis was received by King Aeetes who sacrificed the ram and dedicated the fleece to Zeus. Zeus then transported the ram into the heavens and made it into a constellation.

Taurus (The Bull)

(30 to 60 degrees) 21 April – 21 May

According to Roman legend, Jupiter took the form of a bull and became infatuated with the fair maiden Europa. When Europa decided to ride the bull, it rushed into the sea and whisked Europa off to Crete. Jupiter then raised the bull into the heavens where it became a star.

Gemini (The Twins)

(60 to 90 degrees) 22 May – 21 June

In Greek mythology, Hercules and Apollo are twins. In Roman legend, these twins are said to be Castor and Pollux, the sons of Leda. Pollux was the son of Zeus, who seduced Leda, while Castor was the son of Tyndareus, King of Sparta. Castor and Pollux are mythologically associated with St. Elmo's fire in their role as protectors of sailors. When Castor died, because he was mortal, Pollux begged Zeus to give Castor immortality. Zeus granted the wish by uniting Castor and Pollux together in the heavens as a constellation.

Cancer (The Crab)

(90 to 120 degrees) 22 June-23 July

Roman legend says that Cancer is the crab that bit Hercules during his fight with the Hydra monster. The crab was then placed in the heavens as a star by Juno, the enemy of Hercules.

Leo (The Lion)

(120 to 150 degrees) 24 July – 23 August

Legend says that Hercules battled with the Nemean lion and won. Zeus raised the lion to the heavens as a star.

Virgo (The Virgin)

(150 to 180 degrees) 24 August – 23 September

Legend has it that Virgo is a constellation modelled after Justitia, daughter of Astraeus and Ancora. Justitia lived before mankind sinned. After mankind sinned, Justitia returned to the heavens.

Libra (The Scales)

(180 to 210 degrees) 24 September – 23 October

Libra was known in Babylonian astronomy as a set of scales that were held sacred to the Sun God Shamash, the patron of truth and justice. In Roman mythology, Libra is considered to depict the scales held by Astraea , the Goddess of Justice.

Scorpio (The Scorpion)

(210 to 240 degrees) 24 October – 22 November

According to Greek mythology, Orion boasted to Diana and Latona that he could kill every animal on Earth. The ladies sent for a

17

scorpion which stung Orion to death. Jupiter then raised the scorpion to the heavens as a constellation.

Sagittarius (The Archer)

(240 to 270 degrees) 23 November – 22 December

In Babylonian legend, Sagittarius was the God of War. In Greek legend, Sagittarius was a centaur (half man, half horse) in the act of shooting an arrow. In Roman legend, Sagittarius was a centaur who killed himself when he accidently dropped one of Hercules' poisoned arrows on his hoof.

Capricorn (The Goat)

(270 to 300 degrees) 23 December – 20 January

In Greek legend, during the war with the giants the Greek Gods were driven into Egypt. In order to escape the wrath of the encroaching giants, each Greek God changed his shape. The God Pan leapt into the river Nile and turned the upper part of his body into a goat and the lower part into a fish. This combination was deemed worthy by Jupiter who raised Pan to the heavens.

Aquarius (The Water Bearer)

(300 to 330 degrees) 21 January – 19 February

According to legend, Deucalion- the son of Prometheus, was raised to the heavens after surviving the great deluge that flooded the world.

Pisces (The Fishes)

(330 to 360 degrees) 20 February - 20 March

In Greek legend, Aphrodite and Eros were surprised by Typhon while playing along the river Nile. To escape, they jumped into the water and were changed into two fishes.

Strange Symbols

Figure 3 presents a summary of the symbols used in astrology to denote the various planets and the various aspects. As you repeatedly apply the information in this book to your market activity, you will become quite fluent with these strange looking symbols, called *glyphs*.

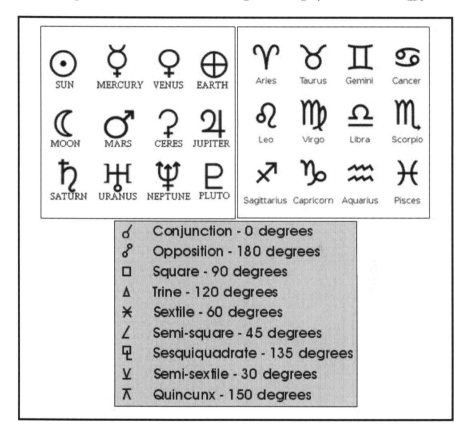

Figure 3 The Glyphs

The Ephemeris

Figure 4 presents a screen shot of a *Geocentric Ephemeris* for the month of December 1980. The ephemeris data in this screen shot has been generated using a software program called Solar Fire Gold. I personally use this program for a lot of my financial astrology work. The symbols denoting the various planets appear along the top of the data table. Along the left axis, the days of the month appear. In each column notice the number expressed in degrees along with a glyph. Thus, for any given day in the month of December 1980, one can find the position of the Moon and the various planets in terms of degrees and astrological sign. For example, on December 1, 1980 we can note that: Jupiter was at 6 degrees Libra. On December 7, Venus was at 16 degrees in the sign of Scorpio. With a little practice, you will quite soon find yourself comfortably interpreting the data in an Ephemeris.

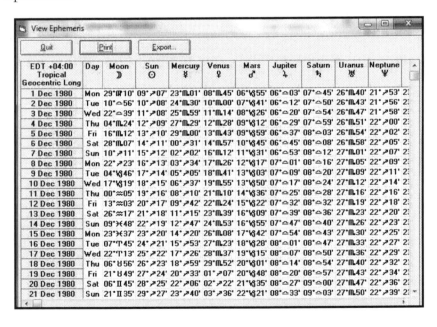

Figure 4 Excerpt from a Geocentric Ephemeris

Solar Fire Gold does a lot more than just generate ephemeris data. I use it to generate and study natal horoscope charts, planetary declination charts and to even quickly search across time for various historical astrological aspects that I am interested in studying. If you are just beginning to dabble in fianncial astrology, there is no pressing immediate urgency to run out and spend the money on Solar Fire Gold. To start with, you can visit your local bookstore and buy an ephemeris book in geocentric format or even in heliocentric format. I suggest one of each.

For geocentric data, I personally have used the *New American Ephemeris for the 21ˢᵗ Century 2000-2100* by Rique Pottenger. To assist you with back testing astrological phenomena, Pottenger also has published the *American Ephemeris 1950-2050* and also the *New American Ephemeris for the 20ᵗʰ Century 1900-2000*.

For heliocentric data, author Neil Michelsen has produced the *American Heliocentric Ephemeris 2001-2050* and also the *American Heliocentric Ephemeris 1901-2000*.

3

ENLIGHTENMENT & PHI

The Golden Mean

The Dark Ages

For thousands of years, mankind has been fascinated with the mathematical relationships between numbers. Some of these numerical relationships are so intriguing that over time they have come to be regarded as sacred. But these treasured documents that described these sacred mathematical relationships nearly came to be lost in 410 AD when the Roman Empire collapsed after Alaric and his Goths sacked the city of Rome. The legions of soldiers and elegant architecture of Rome gave way to a tide of invading barbarians and the Dark Ages set in across the land. Pursuit of knowledge gave way to pursuit of hostility.

Enlightenment

In 600 AD, a society known as the Arabs left Mecca (located in modern day Saudi Arabia) under the inspiration of their leader Mohammed. They ransacked places such as Damascus, Jerusalem and Alexandria taking with them not only the usual spoils of war but also knowledge in the form of old Greek manuscripts. To this ancient Greek knowledge, they added arithmetic and astrological knowledge of the ancient Hindus. By 650 AD, Baghdad had grown to become the cultural epi-center of the East.

Meanwhile, in the West, the remnants of the former Roman Empire came to be reconfigured into the Kingdom of Francia which encompassed much of what is now modern day Europe. In 768 AD, an energetic, charismatic leader by the name of Charlemagne was crowned Emperor of Francia and immediately revived the pursuit of learning and knowledge. The Dark Ages that had spread across the former Roman Empire were finally over.

The pursuit of knowledge was given further impetus in 1000 AD with the election of Pope Sylvester II who revived interest in the seven liberal arts (grammar, rhetoric, logic, arithmetic, geometry, music and astronomy) across the Christian World. Between 1000 AD and 1100 AD, East met West as Arabic knowledge melded with Christian desire for learning. Ancient Greek mathematical works like *Euclid's Elements* were translated into Latin along with various other ancient works.

Filius Bonacci and phi

In 1170 AD, a son was born in Pisa to an Italian merchant and his wife. The merchant's name was Bonacci and the son was named Leonardo. In the language of the day, 'filius' meant 'son of' and before long young Leonardo became known as Filius Bonacci which became shortened to Fibonacci. Leonardo spent much of his youth in Barbary (modern day Spain) where his father operated the Customs House. Leonardo had the great fortune to gain exposure to much of the old Greek and Arabic mathematical knowledge while spending time in Barbary.

In 1202, he published the now famous *Liber Abaci* in which he demonstrated how to solve quadratic equations. Leonardo also became proficient in Pythagorean mathematics and Euclidean geometry. One of the geometrical constructs Leonardo focused on was the Golden Mean.

Figure 5 shows a rectangle divided into two parts (part 'a' and part 'b').

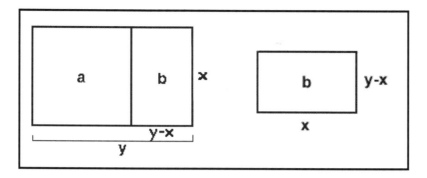

Figure 5 The Golden Mean

There is only one point where this rectangle can be divided into parts 'a' and 'b' such that the following ratio holds:

$$y/x = x/(y-x)$$

To solve this equation one of the variables must be eliminated. So, let x=1. The expression above then becomes:

$$y = 1/(y-1)$$

Multiplying both halves of this expression by (y-1) yields the quadratic expression:

$$y^2-y-1 = 0$$

The one and only viable solution to this quadratic expression is:

$$(1 + \sqrt{5})/2$$

Solving this expression yields 1.618, the *Golden Mean*, also called *phi*, which is denoted by the symbol Φ.

Phi (Φ) is elegant and mystical. Of the mathematical relations known to Greek and Arabic mathematicians, phi (Φ) was probably the most powerful. Hence, its esteemed status as a sacred mathematical term.

The number 1.618 (phi or Φ) derives its name from 5th century BC Greek sculptor Phidas who used it in creating the proportions of the 9 meter high Athena Parthenos statue and the 13 meter high statue of Zeus in BC 430.

English explorer Howard Vyse noted in 1837 that the ancient Egyptians had understood the concept of phi (Φ) long before the Greeks. Vyse observed that the angle of inclination of the pyramid of Cheops is 51 degrees, 51 minutes. Vyse calculated the trigonometric relation 'tangent' of 51 degrees, 51 minutes and arrived at 1.273 which he noted to be the square root of phi (Φ).

When contemplating phi (Φ), it is interesting to study the inverse ratios of it. Figure 6 presents some of these ratios. Notice how these numbers increase by the multiple of 1.618. That is, 0.146 x 1.618 = 0.236 and so on.

RATIOS of Φ		INVERSE RATIOS of Φ	
Φ	1.618	1/ Φ	0.618
Φ^2	2.618	1/ Φ^2	0.382
Φ^3	4.236	1/ Φ^3	0.236
Φ^4	6.854	1/ Φ^4	0.146

Figure 6 Ratios of phi

It is likewise interesting to study the inverse of the square roots of phi as shown in Figure 7.

RATIOS of $\sqrt{\Phi}$		INVERSE RATIOS of $\sqrt{\Phi}$	
$\sqrt{\Phi}$	1.272	$1/\sqrt{\Phi}$	0.786
$\sqrt{\Phi^2}$	1.618	$1/\sqrt{\Phi^2}$	0.618
$\sqrt{\Phi^3}$	2.058	$1/\sqrt{\Phi^3}$	0.486
$\sqrt{\Phi^4}$	2.618	$1/\sqrt{\Phi^4}$	0.382
$\sqrt{\Phi^5}$	3.330	$1/\sqrt{\Phi^5}$	0.300
$\sqrt{\Phi^6}$	4.236	$1/\sqrt{\Phi^6}$	0.236

Figure 7 Inverse ratios of phi

Notice that these numbers increase by a multiple of 1.272 which is the square root of phi (Φ). That is, 0.236 x 1.272 = 0.300 and so on.

Using the Inverse Ratios of phi as part of a Trading Strategy

Stock prices, commodity prices and index values move in distinct waves. In a rising market, buyers - driven by emotion - bid prices higher until the short run marginal benefit of owning the investment is outweighed by the short run marginal economic risk of buying it. Price action then will recede for a period of time before staging another advance.

In a falling market, shareholders sell until price reaches a point where emotion changes and more buyers than sellers are attracted to the investment. Then price action will advance for a period of time as buyers again weigh benefits against risks.

When studying waves of price action on stocks and commodities, the Golden Mean (phi) and its various ratios are often evident. Given the mystical elegance of phi, this should come as no surprise. Consider just how often the Golden Mean can be found in nature. For example, in the human body we have one nose, two eyes and three segments to our limbs. Our arm consists of the segment from the shoulder to the elbow, the segment from the elbow to the wrist and

27

the segment from the wrist to the finger tips. Our leg consists of the segment from the hip to the knee, the segment from the knee to the ankle and the segment from the ankle to the tips of our toes. One, two and three are all related to the Golden Mean as we will explore shortly. As a practical exercise, measure the distance from your wrist to your fingertips. Divide this measurement by the distance from your elbow to your wrist. Examine the resulting number and you will find a ratio of the Golden Mean at work. If the Golden Mean is so prevalent in nature, surely it then stands to reason that it can play a role in the emotional behaviour of buyers and sellers across financial markets

Figure 8 illustrates weekly price action of the Canadian Toronto Stock Exchange (TSX) Composite Index from the March 2009 low to the March 2011 peak and then to the subsequent October 2011 low.

Figure 8 TSX Composite Index and phi

The increase from the 2009 low to the 2011 peak is a move of about 6800 points. The actual figure will vary slightly depending on whether you use the high to low price range or the close to close price range.

The decline into the October 2011 lows was about 3430 points. This decline expressed as a ratio of the increase equates to about 0.5 This figure closely approximates the figure 0.486 which is the inverse ratio of the root of phi (Φ) raised to the 4th power. As this October 2011 sell-off was taking place, many traders and investors who were unaware of esoteric mathematical phenomena were shifting into panic mode. To those that were aware of esoteric math, they saw that this move down was nothing more than an orderly market retracement in harmony with science and nature.

When applying ratios of phi to price moves, bear in mind that the price moves will not be precisely exact to three decimal places. What one should look for is a very close approximation to the ratios along with evidence of a trend change starting to develop as price hits the various respective ratios of phi.

For another example of phi ratios making themselves apparent, consider the long term chart of Gold futures in Figure 9. The price of Gold made a significant low in mid-1999 at the $253/ounce level. This low was re-tested in early 2001 at the $256/ounce level. Prices then ran higher into mid-2012 where they peaked at just over $1900/ounce. Since then, Gold has been struggling to claw its way back up to this level. As Figure 9 illustrates, Gold prices are now trying to hold a support level that corresponds to a 48.6 % retracement of the 2002 to 2012 run-up in price. A failure to hold at this level could see Gold prices retrace even further to the 61.8% level.

Figure 9 Gold Prices and phi

If you do not regularly use such retracements as part of your trading regimen, I encourage you to study price charts across many different time frames. Calculate the price move between two points in time and then express any subsequent retracement move as a ratio and you will very often see phi (Φ) in some form or another making its presence felt. You may see a ratio involving the inverse of phi (Φ) raised to a power 'n'. You may also see a ratio involving the inverse root of phi (Φ) raised to a power 'n'.

The Golden Sequence

Demonstrating the construct of phi (Φ) to post-dark-ages society was significant in itself. But, Fibonacci brought the concept of phi (Φ) to the forefront of 13th century mathematical thinking when he demonstrated its sequential properties. By raising phi (Φ) to a sequence of incrementally higher exponential powers, he demonstrated the construct of what is called the *Golden Sequence* which has unique additive characteristics.

Fibonacci expressed the uniqueness of the Golden Sequence in layman's terms with his story of two rabbits. In his story, a farmer starts with a breeding pair of rabbits (one male and one female) in his field. After month 2, the female rabbit produces a pair of offspring (one male and one female). She produces another pair of offspring each and every month that follows. A given pair of offspring can begin producing pairs of offspring after they are two months old. After the first month, the farmer has only one pair of rabbits. After the second month he will have two pairs. After the third month he will have three pairs of rabbits as the original female gives birth. After the fourth month, the original female produces yet another pair and the female born two months ago produces a pair, giving the farmer five pairs of rabbits. As an interesting exercise, work this rabbit example further to see for yourself the beauty and harmony of the Golden Sequence. This sequence was dubbed the *Fibonacci sequence* by French mathematician Eduard Lucas in the late 1800s.

Table 1 shows the first 24 terms of the sequence which goes 1, 1, 2, 3, 5, 8, 13 ....

Term of Sequence (n)	$F(n)=(1.618)n/\sqrt{5}$	$F(n) / F(n-1)$
1	1	1
2	1	1
3	2	2
4	3	1.5
5	5	1.66
6	8	1.6
7	13	1.625
8	21	1.615
9	34	1.619
10	55	1.617
11	89	1.618
12	144	1.618
13	233	1.618
14	377	1.618
15	610	1.618
16	987	1.618
17	1597	1.618
18	2584	1.618
19	4181	1.618
20	6765	1.618
21	10946	1.618
22	17711	1.618
23	28657	1.618
24	46368	1.618

Table 1 The Fibonacci Sequence

Note that a given term of the sequence is the sum of the two preceding numbers in the sequence. Rounded to the nearest integer, the expression $F(n) = (1.618)^n/\sqrt{5}$ will also produce the various Fibonacci sequence numbers.

Column three of Table 1 shows how the result of dividing a given term of the sequence by the prior term will converge to 1.618 or phi (Φ).

Note also that the sum of any 10 consecutive numbers is divisible by 11. Every 4th term of the sequence is divisible by 3. Every 5th term is divisible by 5. Every 6th term is divisible by 8. These divisors themselves are the corresponding terms of the sequence. For any four consecutive numbers of the sequence, ABC and D, the relation $C^2-B^2 = A \times D$ holds.

Harmonic and beautiful indeed.

The Spiral Calendar™

In my quest to delve deeper into financial astrology, I have come across many unique applications of the Golden Sequence to trading, some of which tie directly to astrology. Perhaps the most elegant such treatment is called the *Spiral Calendar* which was developed and trademarked by former exchange floor trader Christopher Carolan.

Carolan's resulting book entitled the *Spiral Calendar* is a riveting read as he demonstrates the use of Moons as an effective way of measuring time across the history of the financial markets. I highly recommend obtaining a copy of his book.

To demonstrate the power of the Spiral Calendar, Table 2 lists the first 24 terms of the Golden Sequence. The column third from left shows the square root of each of the various Golden Sequence terms. The Spiral Calendar methodology assigns a value of Moons to these square root terms. That is, one Moon cycle is taken as 29.5 days. Multiplying 29.5 by the square root term (column third from left) yields the values in the column at the right (ie the root of the third term of the Golden Sequence is 1.41. 29.5 times 1.41 gives 41.8 days).

Term of Sequence (n)	F(n)=(1.618)n/√5	√F(n)	Days=√F(n) x 29.5
1	1	1	29.5
2	1	1	29.5
3	2	1.41	41.8
4	3	1.73	51.1
5	5	2.24	66.0
6	8	2.83	83.5
7	13	3.61	106.5
8	21	4.58	135.1
9	34	5.83	172.0
10	55	7.42	219.0
11	89	9.43	278.2
12	144	12.00	354.0
13	233	15.26	450.2
14	377	19.42	572.9
15	610	24.70	728.6
16	987	31.42	926.9
17	1597	39.96	1178.9
18	2584	50.83	1499.5
19	4181	64.66	1907.5
20	6765	82.25	2426.4
21	10946	104.62	3086.3
22	17711	133.08	3925.9
23	28657	169.28	4993.8
24	46368	215.33	6352.2

Table 2 Spiral Calendar Counts

Trading the Markets using the Spiral Calendar ™ Technique

Picking up on the example of the TSX Composite Index illustrated in Figure 8, the calendar day count from the March 2009 low to the March 2011 high totals 728 days. Looking at the 15th term of the Golden Sequence in Table 2, one can see it is 610. The square root of 610 is 24.7 Moons or 728.6 days according to Carolan's Spiral Calendar approach. Clearly then, the TSX Composite Index was behaving in harmony with science and nature as it reached its peak in March 2011. The time from the March 2011 peak to the October 2011 low totalled 209 calendar days. A look again at Table 2 shows the 10th term of the Golden Sequence to be 55. The square root of 55 is 7.42 Moons or 219 days according to Carolan's Spiral Calendar approach. Once again, the TSX Composite Index was behaving in very close harmony with science and nature as it declined into its October 2011 low.

The Spiral Calendar can also be seen aligning to the Gold market. As noted, Gold made a significant low in July 1999. This low was successfully re-tested in early 2001. Using this re-test as a starting point, Figure 10 illustrates the application of the Spiral Calendar count using the Market Analyst software platform. When I first started using financial astrology, I would manually mark astrological events and time counts onto charts generated from whatever market data platform I was subscribing to. In 2014, I made the decision to purchase a software package called Market Analyst. It comes complete with a wide range of end of day data. More importantly, it comes complete with a vast array of chart technical analysis tools including an excellent astrology module. I now use Market Analyst for all my charting. It was expensive to purchase, but it was well worth the investment and I strongly recommend this software platform to anyone intent on delving deeply into financial astrology.

Figure 10 Gold Prices and the Spiral Calendar

35

Notice from Table 2 that the 22nd term of the Fibonacci Sequence is 17,711. The square root of this number when multiplied by the 29.5 day lunar cycle yields 3926 days. From the February 20, 2001 price lows, 3926 days takes one to September 21, 2011. The price of Gold hit its peak some 11 days prior. When applying Spiral Calendar counts, one should be looking for evidence that the price trend is changing as the Spiral day-count approaches. Continuing forward in Figure 10, the next significant Spiral day count will come in late-July 2018.

Using the 2011 price high as a starting point for Spiral day counts shows that late-November 2016 will align to 1909 days calculated as the square root of 4148 (the 19th Fibonacci term) multiplied by the lunar cycle of 29.5 days. The next Spiral day count beyond 1907 days is 2426 days. From the 2011 price highs, this count will arrive May 1, 2018. The Spiral count from the 2001 lows suggested late July 2018 would be a significant interval. Combining this timeframe with the count of 2426 days that indicates May 1, 2018 to be significant, leads one to conclude that strict attention must be paid to Gold prices in the May-July, 2018 timeframe.

The Spiral Calendar may also be telling us something about Crude Oil which made a significant price peak in July 2008. The 21st term of the Fibonacci Sequence is 10946. The corresponding Spiral Count is 3089 days. From July 2008, 3089 days places us in mid-December 2016. Oil made a significant low in early 2009 before rallying to another significant peak in April 2011. From this 2011 high, the 19th term of the Fibonacci Sequence aligns to a Spiral Calendar day count of 1909 days which will culminate in July 2016. We could thus likely see Oil finally make its cyclical low early in the second half of 2016.

The Spiral Calendar is a powerful technique to use when trying to forecast future trend changes. With some repeated use, one will soon become very comfortable with the mathematics of it all.

4

SQUARE ROOTS & GANN LINES

W.D. Gann's *Square of Nine* is a concept that is much talked about when it comes to esoteric math and the financial markets. The Square of Nine exemplifies square root mathematics.

The square root of a number 'a' is a number 'y' such that y x y = a. For example, the square root of 16 is 4. If one multiples 4 by itself (4 x 4) the result is 16.

The notion of square roots was well understood by civilizations dating as far back as the ancient Egyptians. W.D. Gann was likely introduced to the Square of Nine concept during his travels in Egypt or India. He did not invent the Square of Nine, but rather used it successfully in his trading. Hence to call it Gann's Square of Nine is misleading. It should simply be called the Square of Nine.

Building the Square of Nine

The Square of Nine is a spiral of numbers expressed on a 2-dimensional grid. The spiral of numbers starts from an apex and then spirals outwards in a clock-wise fashion. The starting apex point for the Square of Nine is the number one. From this starting point, add 1 to each successive number as you travel clockwise.

There are very expensive software programs available to help you generate very elegant Squares of Nine. To date, I have avoided buying such programs, opting instead for the elegant simplicity of a Microsoft Excel spreadsheet. The diagram in Figure 11 illustrates the basic construct of a Square of Nine. In this figure, I stopped my construct after 361, but when building a Square of Nine, one can certainly continue spiralling outwards for many more iterations if desired.

45 degrees — 90 degrees — 135 degrees

307	308	309	310	311	312	313	314	315	316	317	318	319	320	321	322	323	324	325
306	241	242	243	244	245	246	247	248	249	250	251	252	253	254	255	256	257	326
305	240	183	184	185	186	187	188	189	190	191	192	193	194	195	196	197	258	327
304	239	182	133	134	135	136	137	138	139	140	141	142	143	144	145	198	259	328
303	238	181	132	91	92	93	94	95	96	97	98	99	100	101	146	199	260	329
302	237	180	131	90	57	58	59	60	61	62	63	64	65	102	147	200	261	330
301	236	179	130	89	56	31	32	33	34	35	36	37	66	103	148	201	262	331
300	235	178	129	88	55	30	13	14	15	16	17	38	67	104	149	202	263	332
299	234	177	128	87	54	29	12	3	4	5	18	39	68	105	150	203	264	333
298	233	176	127	86	53	28	11	2	1	6	19	40	69	106	151	204	265	334
297	232	175	126	85	52	27	10	9	8	7	20	41	70	107	152	205	266	335
296	231	174	125	84	51	26	25	24	23	22	21	42	71	108	153	206	267	336
295	230	173	124	83	50	49	48	47	46	45	44	43	72	109	154	207	268	337
294	229	172	123	82	81	80	79	78	77	76	75	74	73	110	155	208	269	338
293	228	171	122	121	120	119	118	117	116	115	114	113	112	111	156	209	270	339
292	227	170	169	168	167	166	165	164	163	162	161	160	159	158	157	210	271	340
291	226	225	224	223	222	221	220	219	218	217	216	215	214	213	212	211	272	341
290	289	288	287	286	285	284	283	282	281	280	279	278	277	276	275	274	273	342
361	360	359	358	357	356	355	354	353	352	351	350	349	348	347	346	345	344	343

0 degrees / 360 (left) — 180 degrees (right) — 315 degrees (bottom left) — 270 degrees (bottom) — 225 degrees (bottom right)

Figure 11 The Square of Nine

Support and Resistance using the Square of Nine

There is a great deal of confusion amongst traders and investors as to what the Square of Nine is all about. One does not really need a Square of Nine printout sitting on their desk as they study the markets. What is more important is a good understanding of the mathematical relationships between the numbers in the Square of Nine.

The key to using the Square of Nine is to understand that if one takes the square root of a number that appears in the Square of Nine, adds 2, and re-squares - the resulting number will have taken you on a complete journey around the Square of Nine.

Take a number that you have spotted within the Square of Nine. Take the square root of that number. To this figure, add 0.25. Re-square the resulting sum and round to the nearest whole number. Look at where the result places you in the Square of Nine. Now, repeat this exercise, this time adding 0.5 instead of 0.25. Look at where the result places you within the Square of Nine. Numbers within the square of Nine are related to each other by square root mathematics. Continue to repeat this simple exercise adding 0.75, 1.0, 1.25, 1.50 and eventually 2.0. When it comes to adding 2.0, you will notice that the resulting outcome has taken you on one complete journey around the Square of Nine.

Let's now work an example. Locate the number 11 in the Square of Nine. The number 11 is situated on a horizontal axis called the 0 degree axis that projects from the number 1. The number 1 is the starting point of the Square of Nine. The square root of 11 is 3.3166. Add 0.25 to get 3.5666. Squaring this resulting number gives 12.72, which when rounded to the nearest whole integer gives 13. Take a look at where the number 13 is situated in relation to 11. It is situated on a 45 degree axis that projects from the number 1, the starting point of the Square of Nine.

Continue on with the use of the number 11. Take its square root and add 0.50 to get 3.8166. Square this number and you get 14.56. Rounding up to the nearest whole integer gives 15. The number 15 is situated on a 90 degree axis that projects from the number 1, the starting point of the Square of Nine.

Take the square root of 11 and add 0.75. Re-square the result and you get 17 when rounded up to the nearest whole integer. Look at where 17 is located. It is on the 135 degree axis that projects out from the starting point of the Square of Nine.

Take the root of 11 and add 1.0. Re-square the resulting sum and you get 18.63. Round upwards and you get 19 which is located on the 180

39

degree axis that projects out from the starting point of the Square of Nine.

Take the root of 11 and add 1.5. Re-square the result to get 23.19. Rounding to the nearest integer gives 23 which is located on the 270 degree axis that projects out from the starting point of the Square of Nine.

Lastly take the square root of 11 and add 2. Re-squaring and rounding gives 28. The number 28 is situated on a horizontal axis called the 0 degree axis that projects from the number 1.

So, by taking the square root of a number, adding successively higher increments (0.25, 0.50. 0.75, 1.0, 1.25, 1.50 or 2.0) and re-squaring the result, one can navigate a full 360 degrees around the Square of Nine.

As I noted at the outset, the Square of Nine was not invented by Gann. The power of the square root was well understood by ancient civilizations. Gann merely made the connection between the mathematics of the square root and its harmony with the financial markets.

Traders and investors can follow in Gann's footsteps by using square root mathematics to get a sense of where resistance lines reside for a rising stock or commodity. The Square of Nine can also be used in reverse to determine where lines of support may reside in a falling market. For a given number on the square, take its root, subtract 0.25, 0.50, 0.75, 1.0, 1.25, 1.5 or 2. Re-square the result and round to the nearest integer. See where you end up on the Square.

To make matters easy for yourself, you can construct an Excel spreadsheet to do these square root calculations for you. Set the spreadsheet up so that once you input a price, the spreadsheet uses 0.25, 0.50, 0.75, 1.0, 1.25, 1.5 and 2 to calculate eight different outputs.

Consider the following example. Crude Oil is very much in the news as I craft this manuscript. After hitting a high of at $107 in June 2014, Crude Oil has staged a massive collapse. Market Analyst software has a built-in function to quickly calculate dynamic Square of Nine levels. But, one can also do the same with a simple spreadsheet with a starting point of 1070. Note what I have done here. I have expressed the price of $107 as a 4-digit number, 1070. Taking the root of 1070 gives 32.71. Oil prices have been falling, so one must subtract from 32.71 to determine Square of Nine levels. Subtracting 2 and re-squaring gives 943.15 which can be rounded to 943 or $94.30 per barrel. Next, take the square root of 943, subtract 2 and re-square. The result is 824.31 which can be rounded to 824 or $82.40 per barrel. Doing several more iterations like this takes one down to 282 or $28.20 per barrel. Take the square root of 282 and subtract 0.25. Re-square the result and one gets 273.66 or $27.36 per barrel. My charts show that on January 19, 2016 the March Crude Oil futures contract hit an intra-day low of $27.55 per barrel. Such is the uncanny nature of square root mathematics.

With a simple Excel spreadsheet to do these square root calculations, you can select a chart of your favorite stock or commodity futures contract, look for a significant high or low starting point and then quickly proceed to calculate expected resistance and support levels.

Square root mathematics is a scientific phenomenon that few market participants use or even understand. This valuable methodology can assist you in making more informed investment and trading decisions.

Gann Fan Lines

Another Gann concept that is much talked about is that of *Gann Fan Lines*, sometimes just called Gann lines. I can recall a time when many financial market data providers had a Gann line function built into their charting software suites. Lately, I have noticed that this function does not appear as often as it once did. The reason for this, I suspect, is a general misunderstanding of Gann lines.

Gann lines are a technique in which a starting point of a significant high or low is selected. From this point, angles (vectors) are projected outwards. These vectors are the 1x1, 1x2, 1x4, 1x8 and the 2x1, 4x1 and 8x1.

Many market data software platforms will come with a Gann Fan function already built in. The confusion with Gann lines comes from the mathematical method of constructing the lines. My preference is the methodology used by Daniel Ferrera in his book *Gann for the Active Trader*. Ferrera's method is based on the Gann Square of Nine mathematics.

To illustrate the creation of Gann lines, consider the following example of Gold. On March 17, 2014, Gold made a price high at $1392. This is the point from which I wish to extend Gann lines.

Step 1: Take the price of $1392 and express it as the number 1392. Take the square root of the number 1392 and you get 37.3. This will be your time factor.

Step 2: Subtract 1 from 37.3 and re-square this figure to get 1318.

Step 3: We can now state that our time factor is 37.3 calendar days. We can further state that our price factor is 1392 minus 1318 = $74.

Step 4: From the March 17 date, you will extend a line so that it passes through the time co-ordinate (March 17+37.3 days = April 23) and the price co-ordinate $1318. This line is the Gann 1x1 line.

Step 5: From the March 17 date, you will extend a line so that it passes through the time co-ordinate (March 17+(37.3 x 2) days = May 30) and the price co-ordinate $1318. This line is the Gann 1x2 line.

Step 6: From the March 17 date, you will extend a line so that it passes through the time co-ordinate ((March 17+(0.5) x 37.32) days = April 4) and the price co-ordinate $1318. This line is the Gann 2x1 line.

Step 7: From the March 17 date, you will extend a line so that it passes through the time co-ordinate ((March 17+(0.25) x 37.32) days = March 26) and the price co-ordinate $1318. This line is the Gann 4x1 line.

The Gold price chart in Figure 12 has these Gann lines overlaid starting from the March $1392 high. This chart has been prepared in the Market Analyst software platform, although you can easily follow the methodology shown in this example and overlay Gann lines on a printed chart using a pencil and ruler.

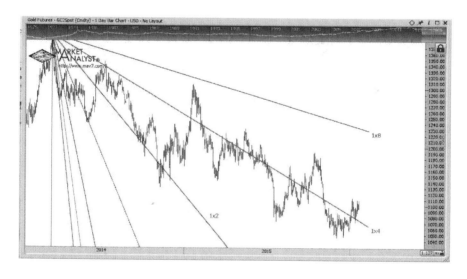

Figure 12 Gann Fan Lines and Gold

Notice from the $1392 high, price action dropped, following the 4x1 line. A rally then pushed price up to the 1x1 line. The rally failed and price fell back to the 2x1 line. A sideways consolidation then ensued for several weeks. A price low was registered right at the 1x1 line. Price then rallied up through the 1x2 line and hit resistance at the 1x4 line. Price then drifted lower and eventually recorded a significant low in the November 2014 timeframe just slightly beneath the 1x2 line. In early 2015, a rally failed just shy of the 1x8 line. As at early 2016, the 1x4 Gann line is providing support and seemingly is proving the general direction for the price trend too. The 1x8 Gann line marks overhead resistance.

To further illustrate Gann Fan lines, consider the price action of the S&P 500 Index which recorded a significant high of 2134 on May 20, 2015.

Step 1: Take the square root of 2134 and you get 46.2. This will be your time factor.

Step 2: Subtract 1 from 46.2 and re-square this figure to get 2042.6

Step 3: We can now state that our time factor is 46 calendar days. We can further state that our price factor is 2134 minus 2042 = 92.

Step 4: From the May 20, 2015 date, you will extend a line so that it passes through the time co-ordinate (May 20+ 46 days = July 4) and the price co-ordinate 2042. This line is the Gann 1x1 line.

Step 5: From the May 20 date, you will extend a line so that it passes through the time co-ordinate (May 20+(46 x 2) days = August 19) and the price co-ordinate 2042. This line is the Gann 1x2 line.

The math is really quite straightforward for all of the Gann Fan lines once you identify the starting point and use Daniel Ferrera's method involving squares and square roots.

Figure 13 illustrates the application of Gann Fan lines to a chart of the S&P 500 using a starting point of May 20, 2015. The 1x8 line has acted as overhead resistance since the 2015 high. The early 2016 sell-off severely tested the 1x2 line and price action is now attempting to hold onto this support.

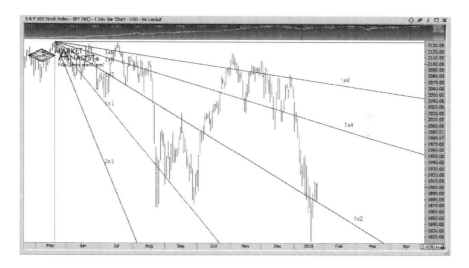

Figure 13 – S&P 500 and Gann Fan Lines

Gann Planetary Transit Lines

There is one other Gann concept whose power continues to amaze me – even though this concept is not talked about much anymore by technical chartists. The technique I refer to is *Gann Planetary Transit Lines*.

In order to fully implement this technique, one must become comfortable with the notion of expressing degrees of planetary motion, as determined from the zodiac wheel, in terms of price. At first blush, the visceral instinct is to say that degrees of motion are in no way, shape or form related to price. But, thanks to the works of

W.D. Gann there is a way to accomplish the conversion of degrees to price and it is called the *Wheel of 24*.

Transit lines involve taking the longitudinal position of a given planet and converting that longitude to price by means of the Wheel of 24 (also known as the *Universal Clock*). Figure 14 illustrates the Wheel of 24. The image for this Figure has been gleaned from one of Jeanne Long's publications that is no longer in print. Ms. Long took the basic concept of the Wheel of 24 as posited by Gann and trademarked it as her Universal Clock, hence the trademark notation in the title at the bottom left of the image. Find any of Jeanne Long's old publications and you will be able to read more about her Universal Clock.

Transit lines are plotted for Mars, Jupiter, Saturn, Uranus and Neptune. Once the transit lines have been calculated and plotted, one can then overlay price data on the chart.

The Wheel of 24 (Universal Clock) is divided into an inner ring and an outer ring. The rings are divided into 24 segments. The inner ring displays the numbers 1 through 360 with these numbers advancing by an increment of 1 in a counter-clockwise direction. These numbers denote the 360 degrees of the zodiac. The outer ring presents price data. From the 90 degree position where the number 1 appears, move right until you hit the outer ring. This is where the first entry of the price data will appear. Generally, the price data entries will be structured so that from lowest to highest the data takes into account the entire price range of the stock or commodity over the past year. The price data advances by a suitably chosen increment so that in about 10 or so revolutions of the Wheel of 24, the desired price range can be expressed.

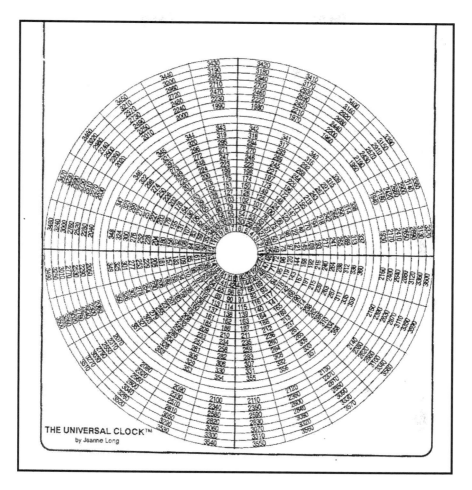

Figure 14 The Universal Clock

As an example, suppose one wanted to add the Uranus transit lines to a chart of Crude Oil futures for the period 2011 through 2014. On a piece of paper, make a rough sketch of a wheel divided into 24 segments. Arrange the sequential numbers on the inner ring of the wheel starting at 1 and ending at 360. You could start the numbering sequence of the outer wheel at $0 and make each of the 24 increments higher by $0.10. One revolution of the outer wheel will take the price from $0 to $2.40. Obviously the price of Crude Oil is much higher than $2.40. To facilitate an easier analysis, start the scale of the outer wheel at $96 (40 revolutions x $2.40) and add $0.10 to each segment. One complete revolution of the wheel will take your price to $98.40. A total of five revolutions from your start point will take you to a price of $108.40.

Consider that at February 1, 2011, Uranus was at a heliocentric degree position of 0 Aries, or 0 degrees of the zodiac. In your sketched wheel, find 0 degrees on the inner portion of the wheel. Notice that this corresponds to $96, $98.40, $100.80, $103.20, $105.60 and $108.00 on the outer wheel segment. On a chart of Crude Oil, make a mark at February 1, 2011 and each of $96, $98.40, $100.80, $103.20, $105.60 and $108.00. Next, note that at February 18, 2014 Uranus was at a heliocentric location of 12 Aries or 12 degrees of the zodiac. On your sketched wheel, locate the number 12 on the inner wheel and see what outer wheel prices correspond to that point. You will find the corresponding points to be $97.20, $99.60, $102.00, $104.40, $106.80, and $109.20. On your Crude Oil chart, make a mark at February 18, 2014 and each of $97.20, $99.60, $102.00, $104.40, $106.80, and $109.20.

Join these respective points to the February 1, 2011 points and you will have generated a series of Uranus transit lines. Notice that the Crude Oil price highs in 2012 and 2013 were generally constrained by this Uranus transit line. Extend the slope of this Uranus line into the future and you now have a valuable tool for assessing overhead price resistance.

To complete this exercise of creating transit lines, make every fourth line the same color (I typically use green). Make the intermediate lines a separate color (I use red). The fourth lines (green) will be those at $9.60, $19.20, $28.80, $38.40, $48, $57.6, $67.20, $76.8, $86.4, $96, $105.60. These are what Jeanne Long refers to as the transit lines. The intermediate divisions are what she terms harmonics.

Doing transit lines manually can be tedious work. Market Analyst software has a built in function that allows the user to generate transit lines with the click of a mouse. Figure 15 illustrates a chart of Crude Oil prices to which I have added the Uranus transit lines and the intermediate harmonics. Figure 15 illustrates that Crude Oil as of early 2016 had found support at a harmonic level underneath a transit line.

Figure 15 Crude Oil and Uranus Transit Lines

To further illustrate the power of transit lines, consider the chart in Figure 16 of the Dow Jones Industrial Average. Note how the Dow Jones found support at a Mars transit line in August 2015. Price action in early 2016 came within 100 points of touching a Mars harmonic line.

Figure 16 Dow Jones Average and Mars Transit Lines

And lastly, consider one last example of the Eurocurrency. Figure 17 illustrates Euro price action with heliocentric Jupiter transit lines overlaid. To manually create these Jupiter lines, one would construct the Universal Clock so that each of the 24 segments corresponded to a price increment of 0.004166. One complete revolution of the wheel will then be 0.10 (0.00416 x 24 = 0.10).

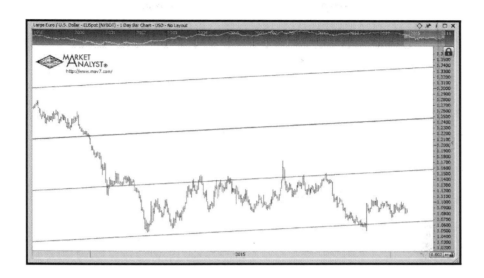

Figure 17 Eurocurrency and Jupiter transit lines

Notice that during 2015, a Jupiter transit line harmonic has been acting as support. A break of this transit line support in 2016 could spell trouble for the Eurocurrency.

5

QUANTUM PRICE LINES

In the early 1700s philosopher and scientist Sir Isaac Newton developed his theory of *Universal Gravitation* which claimed that planets in our solar system are attracted to one another by gravity. Newton further said that space and time were absolute and that the world functioned according to an absolute order. Furthermore, he said that space was a three-dimensional entity and time was a two-dimensional entity.

In the early 1900s, Albert Einstein advanced his *Theory of Relativity* that posited Newton's notion of time and space was outdated. Einstein said the passage of time of an object was related to its speed with respect to that of another observer. Thus was penned the concept of relative space-time in which space was not uniform.

Einstein further stated that relative space-time could be distorted depending on the density of matter. That is, space-time in the area of the Sun is more distorted because the Sun has a great, huge mass. Light particles travelling near the Sun are then pulled away from their linear path due to the mass of the Sun.

Quantum Price Lines are based on this space-time theory. The whole notion of quantum lines posits that the price of a stock, index or commodity can be thought of as a light particle or as an electron that can occupy different energy levels which physicists call orbital shells. These energy levels are the price levels that we recognize as being support or resistance on a price chart.

Author Fabio Oreste has done a masterful job of taking quantum physics and space-time theory and blending both with the curvature mathematics of 19th century mathematician Bernhard Riemann. Oreste applied the outcome of his work to price charting. In his work, price is considered to be akin to light particles. These light particles are then deflected by actions of planets. This deflection is what gives us price highs and lows on a chart.

Oreste has taken the Gann Transit Line notion and married it to modern physics. His book, entitled *Quantum Trading*, is a worthy resource for any investor.

The Oreste formula for quantum price line calculation is :

$$\text{Quantum Line} = (N \times 360) + PSO \ ;$$

Where PSO = heliocentric planetary longitude x Conversion Scale
Where N = the harmonic level (1,2,4,8...)
Where Conversion Scale = 2^n ; 1,2,4,8,16 ....

When dealing with prices less than 360, the inverse variation of the formula is used.

$$\text{Quantum Line} = (1/N \times 360) + PSO$$

Once one has calculated a Quantum Line, one can then apply a multiplication factor to generate sub-divisions. Multiplication factors are in increments of 0.0625 (1.000, 1.0625, 1.125....all the way to 1.9375).

Oreste advises to start with applying Pluto Quantum Lines to a price chart. Look to see that the lines correspond to significant highs or lows. If Pluto lines are not adequate, next examine Neptune lines, Uranus lines and Saturn lines.

Consider the following two examples:

S&P 500 Index

I have found that the Pluto quantum lines (Conversion Scale=2, N=2) work quite well for the S&P 500 Index.

During 2015, consider that heliocentric Pluto was at 13 degrees of Capricorn (283 degrees of the zodiac) on January 1 and at 15 degrees Capricorn (285 degrees of the zodiac) on December 31. The suite of Quantum Lines for January 1, 2015 would be created as:

$$\text{Quantum Line} = (N \times 360) + PSO$$
$$\text{Quantum Line} = (2 \times 360) + (2 * 283) = 1286$$

Sub-division lines would be at 1286 x 1.0625, 1286 x 1.125 and so on.

The calculations for the December 31 time point would be similar except the heliocentric position of Pluto would be 285 degrees.

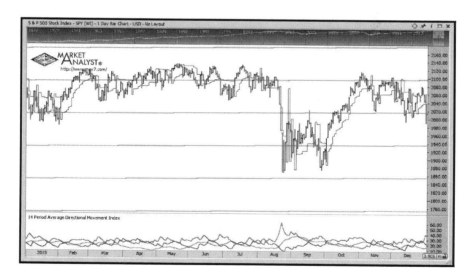

Figure 18 – S&P 500 with Pluto Quantum Lines

Figure 18 illustrates price action for the S&P 500 Index in 2015. I have used the Market Analyst built-in Quantum Line function to overlay the Quantum Lines onto the chart, although one could have generated the lines manually as well. Note how for much of 2015, a Pluto line marked resistance for the S&P 500. In August and September another Pluto line acted as support.

Corn Futures

I have found that the inverse Pluto quantum lines (Conversion Scale of 1/4, N=1/2) work quite well for studying Corn futures.

During 2015, consider that heliocentric Pluto was at 13 degrees of Capricorn (283 degrees of the zodiac) on January 1 and at 15 degrees Capricorn (285 degrees of the zodiac) on December 31. The suite of Quantum Lines for January 1, 2015 would be created as:

Quantum Line = (1/N x 360) + PSO

Quantum Line = (360/4) + (283/2) = 231.5

Sub-division lines would be at 231.5 x 1.0625, 231.5 x 1.125 and so on.

The calculations for the December 31 time point would be similar except the heliocentric position of Pluto would be 285 degrees.

Figure 19 illustrates price action for Corn futures in 2015. I have used the Market Analyst built-in Quantum Line function to overlay the Quantum Lines onto the chart, although one could have generated the lines manually as well. Note in mid-2015 a Pluto line marked overhead resistance for Corn futures at the $4.35/bushel level. Price then fell sharply and eventually found support at a Pluto line at the $3.50/bushel level.

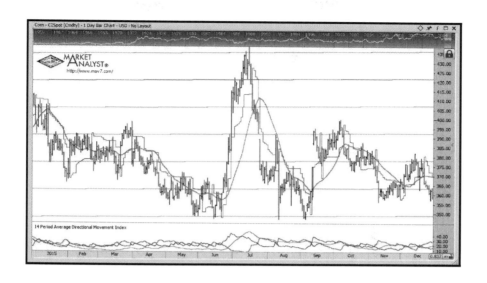

Figure 19 - Corn Futures and Quantum Lines

Table 3 presents a listing of various commodities and equity indices along with the Conversion Scale figures and N settings that I use in my market studies.

Commodity or Index	Planet	Conversion Scale	N
Nasdaq Composite Index	Pluto	8	2
Dow Jones Industrials	Pluto	32	2
FTSE 100 Index	Pluto	16	2
German Dax Index	Pluto	16, 32	2
Gold Futures	Pluto	1	2
Silver Futures	Pluto	1/64	1/64
Canadian Dollar, Australian dollar, Japanese Yen Futures	Pluto	1/1024	1/1024
Eurocurrency, British Pound Futures	Pluto	1/512, 1/1024	1/512, 1/1024
Wheat & Corn Futures	Pluto	1/128, 1/256	1/128, 1/256
Soybean Futures	Pluto	1/64, 1/128	1/64, 1/128
WTI Crude Oil Futures	Pluto	1/32, 1/16	1/32, 1/16
Sugar Futures	Pluto	1/64, 1/32	1/64, 1/32
Cocoa Futures	Pluto	4, 8	2
30 Year Bond Futures	Saturn	1/4, 1/8	1/4, 1/8
10 Year Treasury Futures	Pluto	1/8	1/8

Table 3 – Quantum Line Calculation Factors

6

THE MOON

Look skyward on any clear night and you will see the Moon in one of its various phases. The Moon is the closest of all the planetary bodies to the Earth and has long been held in fascination by mankind.

Throughout the centuries, the Moon has been associated with changing mood or health. In 6th century Constantinople (modern day Istanbul, Turkey), physicians at the court of Emperor Justinian advised that gout could be cured by inscribing verses of Homer on a copper plate when the Moon was in the sign of Libra or Leo. In 17th century France, astrologers used the Moon to explain mood changes in women. In 17th century England, herbal remedy practitioners advised people to pluck the petals of the peony flower when the Moon was waning. During the Renaissance period, it was thought that dreams could come true if the Moon was in the signs of Taurus, Leo, Aquarius or Scorpio.

Today, the Moon continues to be recognized as a powerful celestial body. Talk to any hospital professional or psychological therapist about the Full Moon and you are sure to hear plenty of stories about human behaviour being erratic at these times of the lunar cycle. Just as the gravitational pull of the Moon can influence the action of tides, it somehow also influences our emotions. On a short term basis, as our emotions change, our investment buying and selling decisions also change. The tangible result can be a change in price trend action. On a longer term basis, the Moon can be seen to influence not only financial markets but real estate markets and entire economies as well

Lunar Phases and the Synodic Month

Much like the planets orbit the Sun, the Moon orbits the Earth. The Moon orbits the 360 degrees around the Earth in a plane of motion called the *lunar orbit plane*. This orbit plane is inclined at about 5 degrees to the ecliptic plane of the Earth. The Moon orbits Earth with a slightly elliptical pattern in approximately 27.3 days, relative to an observer on a fixed frame of reference like the Sun. This time period is known as a *sidereal month*. However, during one sidereal month, an observer located on Earth (a frame of reference that moves around the Sun) will himself revolve part of the way around the Sun. To that observer, a complete orbit of the Moon around the Earth will appear longer than the sidereal month at approximately 29.5 days. This 29.5 day period of time is known as a *synodic month* or more commonly a *lunar month*. Recall from Chapter 3 that the lunar month time period was used in the Spiral Calendar calculations.

The North Node of Moon Changing Signs

The lunar orbit plane being inclined at about 5 degrees to the Earth's ecliptic plane means these planes are not parallel. Mathematically, two planes that are not parallel must intersect. The intersection points between the Moon's plane and Earth's ecliptic are termed the *North Node* and the *South Node*. Astrologers tend to focus on the North Node and Ephemeris tables will clearly list the zodiac position of the North Node for each calendar day. Study the North Node positions and you will see that it moves in a backwards, retrograde pattern through the zodiac. The length of time for the North Node to make a full journey through the 12 signs of the zodiac is 18.6 years.

As part of a trading or investing strategy, consider noting the times when the North Node changes signs of the zodiac, approximately every 1.55 years. The S&P 500 Index has a propensity to deliver trend changes as the North Node changes signs of the zodiac. In early January 2014 the S&P 500 recorded a sharp drop of over 100 points as the Node was about to move from Scorpio into Libra. Between early September and late October, 2012 the S&P 500 sold off over 100 points as the North Node moved from Sagittarius into Scorpio. In March 2011 a 100 point sell off occurred as Node moved from Capricorn into Sagittarius. In June 2006 the S&P 500 began to rally in a meaningful way after the Node moved from Aries into Pisces. This strength started to fail in a serious way in December 2007 as Node moved from Pisces into Aquarius. More recently, the severe weakness in early 2016 aligns exactly to the Node moving from Libra into Virgo.

The North Node and the Business Cycle

In 1938, author and trader Louise McWhirter published her book, *McWhirter Theory of Stock Market Forecasting*. One of the more fascinating sections of her book deals with the general business cycle and the North Node of the Moon. She posits that the general economy will move in a 18.6 year business cycle in harmony with the 18.6 year synodic period of the North Node. As the North Node moves into the sign of Taurus, the general economy will slow down. This below normal economic behavior will last for about three years until the Node passes out of the sign of Aquarius.

Aquarius is considered to be the bottom of the economic cycle. Remember, the Node will be seen to move in a backwards retrograde motion from our vantage point here on Earth. Interestingly, in late 1928 the Node transited into Taurus which signalled a slowdown. Some nine months later, the stock market crashed and a harsh economic climate set in.

As the Node moves through Capricorn and Sagittarius, the economy will pick up momentum again. Through Scorpio and Libra, the general economy will approach a very high level of activity with a peak in activity coming as the Node leaves the sign of Leo. As the

Node then moves through the signs of Cancer and Gemini, economic activity is positive but beginning to slow to more normal levels. Of course, the caveat to this cycle behavior is external political and socioeconomic events that may arise unexpectedly.

Real estate analysts and economists who follow the rigors of astrology, have noted that this business cycle behavior can be seen in the real estate market, not just in the USA, but globally. In 2006, global real estate markets peaked in terms of re-sale price and overall demand. In June 2006, the Node moved into the sign of Pisces. In December 2007, the Node moved into the sign of Aquarius. In reflection, the 1.55 year period commencing in late 2007 was indeed a dark hour for the global real estate industry and for the global economy in general.

The Node entered Virgo in early January 2016. While the economy still bears battle scars from the 2007-2008 downturn, it is easy to see that activity continues to build. Barring any major upsets with Euro-zone cohesiveness or stability in other parts of the globe, the general economy should continue to improve until the Node transits out of Leo in late 2018. After 2018, the economy will gradually decline until the 18.6 year cycle completes itself. Keep your focus on 2026 and 2027. This is when the current 18.6 year economic cycle will make its bottom. In a world of artificial stimulus and economic uncertainty, if you thought the 2008 financial crisis was nasty, we may be in for an even bigger event in 2026-2027.

Solar and Lunar Eclipses

A *solar eclipse* occurs when the Moon passes between the Sun and Earth and fully or partially blocks the Sun. This can happen only at a New Moon, when the Sun and the Moon are in conjunction and only when the New Moon occurs close to one of the Nodes. Because the Moon's lunar orbit plane intersects with the ecliptic plane at the two Nodes that are 180 degrees apart, eclipses occur at New Moons close to the nodes at two periods of the year approximately six months

(173.3 days) apart, known as *eclipse seasons*. There will always be at least one solar eclipse during an eclipse season. Sometimes the New Moon occurs close enough to a node during each of two consecutive months to eclipse the Sun in two partial eclipses. This means that in any given year, there will always be at least two solar eclipses, but there could be as many as five.

A *lunar eclipse* occurs when the Sun, Earth, and Moon are aligned exactly, or very closely so, with the Earth in the middle. The Earth blocks the Sun's rays from striking the Moon. This can only happen at a Full Moon. Lunar eclipse dates should be watched for closely as price trend changes often can occur at these times. The chart in Figure 20 illustrates price behaviour of the S&P 500 futures going back to late 2014.

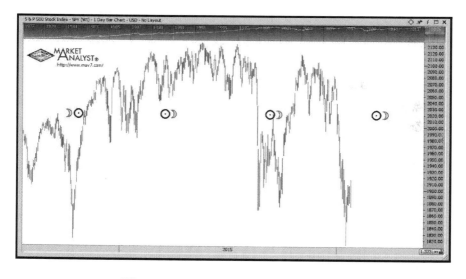

Figure 20- S&P 500 and Eclipses

The Sun and Moon icons denote eclipse events. October 14, 2014 marked a significant low on the S&P 500. This low was bracketed by a lunar eclipse on October 8 and a solar eclipse on October 23. September 17, 2015 marked a sharp reversal on the S&P 500. This reversal was preceded by a solar eclipse four days earlier. September

29, 2015 marked another sharp reversal. Two days previous, there had been a lunar eclipse.

Volatility and the Moon

In 2004, the Chicago Board Options Exchange created a tradable instrument to measure the implied volatility of S&P 500 Index options. This instrument has become very popular with both traders and the media alike and it is most often referred to by the name '*VIX*'. At any given time, what the VIX tells traders and investors is the expected volatility on the S&P Index for the following 30 days.

For example, if the VIX has a reading of 15 on a particular day, then traders should expect the S&P 500 Index to exhibit volatility of $15/\sqrt{12} = 4.33\%$ over the following 30 days. The impact of the Moon can be seen when studying the VIX. Figure 21 is a daily chart of VIX price action from August 2015 to January 2016. New Moon events and Full Moon events have been marked on this chart. The solid circles denote New Moons and the lighter circles denote Full Moons. Traders with short term time horizons may be interested to notice that the VIX tends to record inflection points at New Moon and Full Moon events.

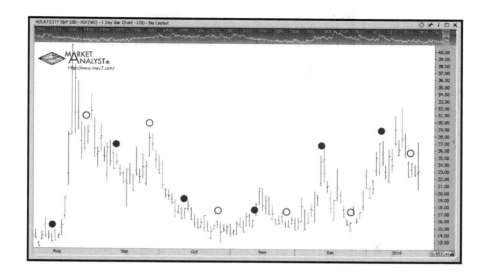

Figure 21 – VIX and Moons

Moon Phases and Price Inflection Points

Not every stock or commodity future will respond equally to Moon phases. In my experience, it is important to examine past price behavior of a stock in relation to Moon phases to see if the stock has a propensity to react at changes in Moon phase.

Figure 22 presents a price chart for J.P. Morgan (NYSE: JPM) for the last part of 2015. The chart has been overlaid with a short term moving average and New Moon events. Note that the New Moon events align to short term inflection points. A nimble day-trader using hourly charts might be able to take advantage of these price inflections.

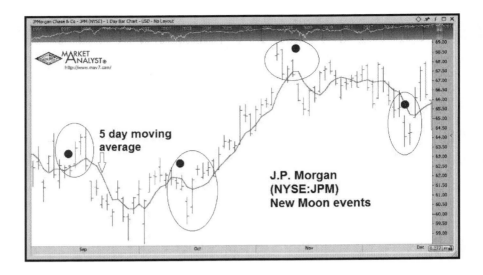

Figure 22 – J.P. Morgan (JPM) and New Moon events

7

MERCURY

Mercury is the smallest planet in our solar system. Mercury is also the closest planet to the Sun. As a result of its proximity to the powerful gravitational pull of the Sun, Mercury moves very quickly – completing an orbit of the Sun in 88 days. As Figure 23 shows, the orbit of Mercury is not circular, but rather somewhat elliptical.

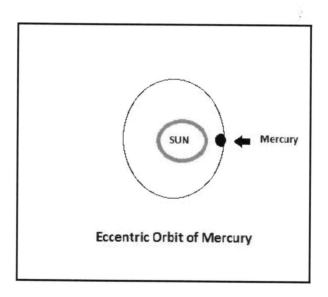

Figure 23 – Elliptical Orbit of Mercury

This elliptical orbit can be better quantified by considering the *Elongation* of Mercury. Elongation refers to the angle between the planet and the Sun, using Earth as a reference point, as Figure 24 shows.

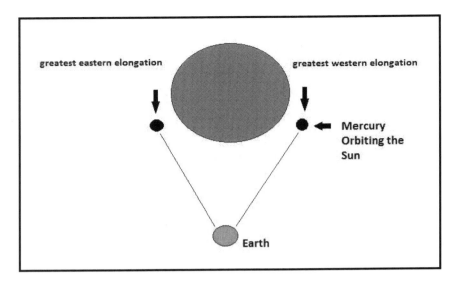

Figure 24 – Elongation of Mercury

Scientists have determined that Mercury's elliptical orbit will place it at a range of 46 million kms to 70 million kms from the Sun. When Mercury is *nearer* to the Sun (ie. 46 million kms away), it is moving at its fastest (~56.6 kms per second). When Mercury is *farther* from the Sun (ie. 70 million kms away), it is moving slower (~38.7 kms per second). The point where it is nearest to the Sun is called *Perihelion.* The point where it is farthest from the Sun is called *Aphelion.*

When studying Mercury and its impact on financial astrology, one must also consider the Superior and Inferior Conjunctions of Mercury. When Mercury is between the Earth and the Sun, it is in *Inferior Conjunction.* When Sun is between Earth and Mercury, then Mercury is said to be at *Superior Conjunction.* It helps to think of Mercury at Inferior Conjunction as being the start of a new 88 day heliocentric cycle. Figure 25 illustrates these conjunctions.

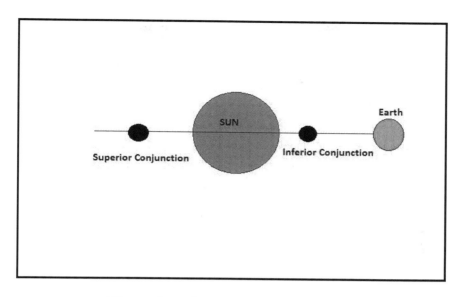

Figure 25 – Conjunctions of Mercury

Lastly, when studying Mercury and the financial markets, one must look at the Retrograde action of Mercury. Consider the diagram in Figure 26.

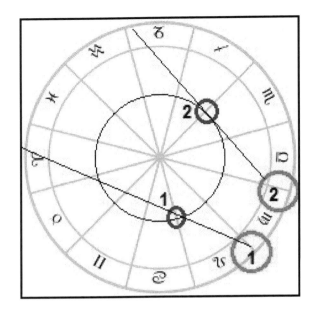

Figure 26 – Mercury Retrograde

In 30 days of time, planet Earth (shown as the larger circles in the diagram) will travel 30 degrees of the zodiac (from point 1 to point 2). But, Mercury is a faster mover. In the same 30 days of time, Mercury (shown as smaller circles) will travel through about 120 degrees of the zodiac (point 1 to point 2) – passing by Earth in the process.

From our vantage point here on Earth, initially as Mercury is setting up to pass Earth, we see Mercury in the sign of Aries. As Mercury completes its trip past Earth, we see it in the sign of Capricorn. In other words, the way we see it here on Earth, Mercury has moved backwards from Aries to Capricorn as it passed Earth. This is the concept of Retrograde. To the ancients who did not fully understand how the cosmos worked, it must have been awe-inspiring to see a planet move backwards in the heavens.

To fully appreciate Mercury and its various features, it helps to look at a few examples.

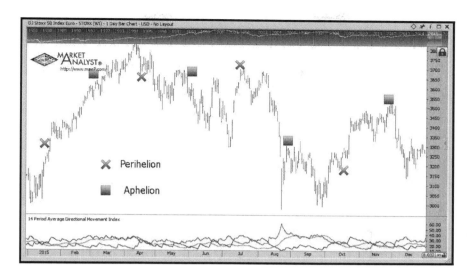

Figure 27 – Mercury Perihelion and Aphelion

Figure 27 illustrates the price action of the Stoxx 50 Index for 2015 with Mercury Perihelion and Aphelion events overlaid. Study this chart closely and you will see quite a good alignment between trend changes confirmed by the DMI technical indicator and Perihelion events. The bottom of a violent sell-off in August, 2015 came mere days ahead of a Mercury Aphelion event. A trend change and an interim high came in November at another Aphelion event.

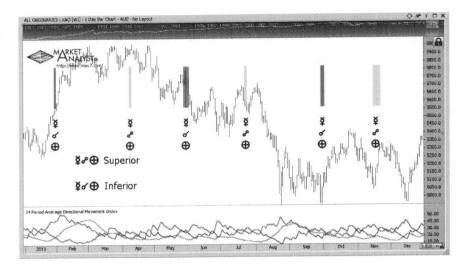

Figure 28 – Mercury Superior and Inferior Conjunctions

Figure 28 illustrates the price action of the Australian All Ordinaries Index (XAO) during 2015 with Mercury Superior and Inferior conjunction events overlaid. A Superior event in early April 2015 aligned to a significant market high and a trend change. A Superior event in July was a precursor to a significant sell-off. An Inferior event in late September marked a double-bottom market low.

Figure 29 illustrates price action of Gold futures during 2015 with Mercury greatest east and west elongation events overlaid.

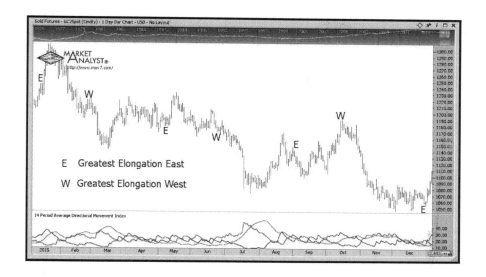

Figure 29 – Mercury Elongations

In this chart note that the price high for 2015 was recorded a handful of days after a Mercury greatest easterly elongation event. An attempt at a meaningful price rally was stopped dead in its tracks in October at a westerly elongation event. An easterly elongation event in December marked the price low for 2015 and the start of a brief rally into early 2016.

Figure 30 illustrates price action for the Nasdaq 100 Index during 2015 with Mercury Retrograde events overlaid.

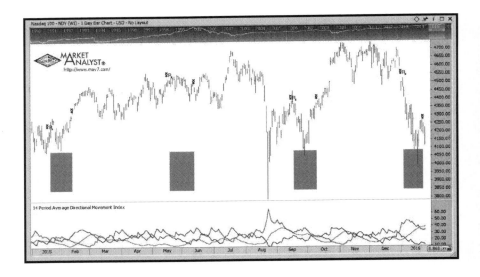

Figure 30 – NASDAQ 100 and Mercury Retrograde

Note that a trend change developed in February 2015 at a Mercury Retrograde event. A sell-off and subsequent trend change in September occurred during a Retrograde event. The end of a violent sell-off came to an end in early 2016 at a Retrograde event.

Mercury might be a small planet, but is has many features to consider. If using Mercury as a tool to help you navigate a market index or a particular stock or commodity, look at all the various Mercury features discussed in this chapter. And remember, you are looking for a Mercury feature or event to align with a short term trend change where the trend change is evidenced by a suitable chart technical indicator.

8

VENUS

Venus is the second planet from the Sun. It is of similar size and mass to planet Earth and orbits the Sun in 225 days.

When Venus is between the Earth and the Sun, it is in Inferior Conjunction. When Sun is between Earth and Venus, then Venus is said to be at Superior Conjunction.

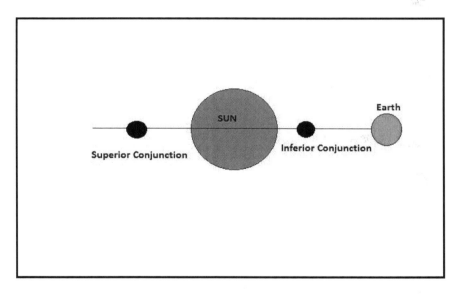

Figure 31 – Venus Conjunctions

To an observer situated on Earth, Venus will be visible as a morning star for 263 days after it has completed its Inferior Conjunction. The 263 days after Venus has completed its Superior Conjunction will see it visible as an evening star to an observer on Earth. When Venus is precisely at Inferior Conjunction, an observer on Earth will not be able to see it for about eight days because it will be obscured by the Sun. When Venus is precisely making its Superior Conjunction, there will be a 50 day period when it will not be visible to an observer on Earth.

Thus, to an observer on Earth, the total Venus cycle will be (8+263 +50+263 = 584 days).

The times when Venus changes from being visible as a morning star to being visible as an evening star are significant events that investors should pay close attention to as markets do have a propensity to exhibit trend changes at these events.

The best way to appreciate Venus is to look at some examples.

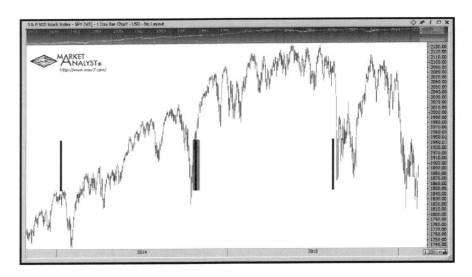

Figure 32 – Venus Superior and Inferior Conjunctions

Figure 32 illustrates price behavior of the S&P 500 Index going back to mid-2013. In early 2014, the S&P 500 started the year with a stiff sell-off which panicked many investors. This event was simply Venus changing from being visible as an evening star to being visible as a morning star at Inferior Conjunction. In late 2014, another violent sell-off rocked the S&P 500. The market stabilized and started to rise again mere days ahead of a Superior Conjunction. The violent sell-off in August 2015 was an Inferior Conjunction event.

Traders and investors should also pay close attention to the 225 day heliocentric journey of Venus around the Sun. Markets often exhibit trend changes in harmony with this journey.

Figure 33 illustrates price behavior of the S&P 500 from late 2014 to early 2016. The heliocentric 225 day intervals of Venus have been overlaid on the chart using a starting point of March 9, 2009 which by all measures was an extremely significant event. Note that the end of a 225 day heliocentric cycle marked a precipice for the S&P 500 in October 2014. Just over 225 days later, in mid-May, 2015 the S&P 500 recorded a significant high which at this time of writing has not been seen since. One 225 day heliocentric cycle later (plus a few days) marked another precipice for the S&P 500 which saw a massive sell-off.

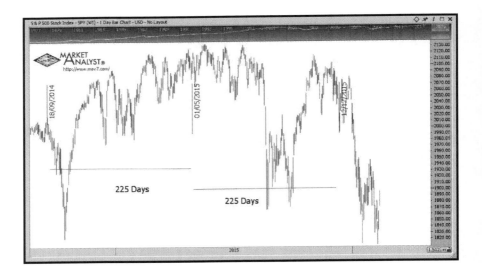

Figure 33 – Venus 225 day heliocentric cycle

The geocentric cycle of Venus where it appears as morning and evening stars over the 584 day cycle is probably the most powerful Venus cycle to pay attention to. However, the 225 day heliocentric cycle is also worthy of note.

To assist you with some back-testing, consider that Venus was at Inferior Conjunction on January 15, 2006, August 18, 2007, March 29, 2009, October 29, 2010, June 6, 2012, January 11, 2014, August 15, 2015. The next Inferior event will be March 25, 2017.

Venus was at Superior Conjunction on October 27, 2006, June 9, 2008, January 11, 2010, August 16, 2011, March 28, 2013, October 26, 2014. The next Superior event will be June 7, 2016.

From mid-December 2015, the next Venus heliocentric cycle will come due July 24, 2016 and again on March 6, 2017.

9

DECLINATION

Declination refers to the positioning of a celestial body above or below the Earth's celestial equator plane. Celestial bodies experience declinations of up to about 25 degrees above and below the celestial equator plane.

My market back-testing research has revealed that changes in the declination of a celestial body can affect the human psyche. Why this happens remains a mystery to me.

Moon, Mercury, Venus, Mars and indeed Earth itself endure frequent changes in declination due to the gravitational force of the Sun. Planets like Jupiter, Saturn, Neptune, Uranus and Pluto also experience declination changes but these changes are slow to evolve.

To generate declination plots, I use the software program *Solar Fire Gold*. Figure 34 presents an example of a declination plot for 2014 through 2015.

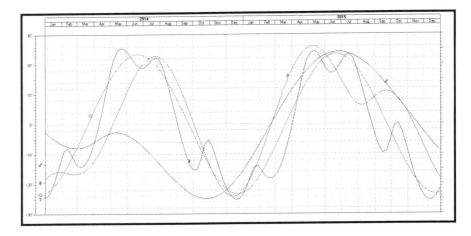

Figure 34 – Declination Plot

In my back-testing, I have noted that the declination of Venus seems to deliver the most consistent correlations to price inflections.

Following are two examples that illustrate the declination of Venus to market price inflection points.

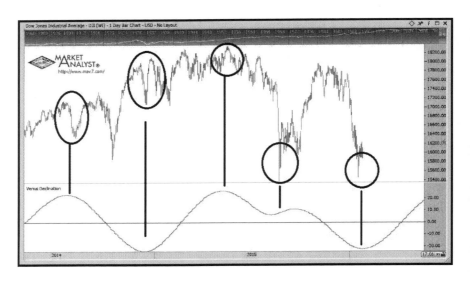

Figure 35 – Dow Jones Average and Venus Declination

Figure 35 illustrates price action on the Dow Jones Average for late 2014 through to early 2016. The Venus declination plot has been added to the lower pane of this chart. Notice how inflection points of Venus declination align to inflection points on the Dow Jones.

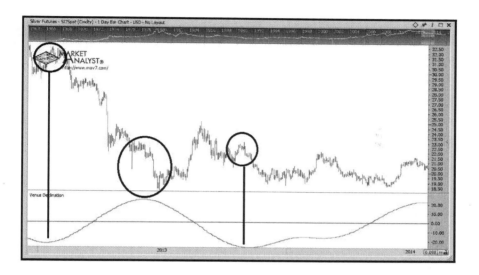

Figure 36 – Silver and Venus Declination

Figure 36 illustrates Silver futures price action for 2013 and much of 2014. I have added the Venus declination plot as a separate pane on the chart.

The declination of the Moon is also a powerful tool to utilize. It is well known that W.D. Gann was a proponent of using the declination of Moon to assist with trading decisions.

The chart in Figure 37 illustrates price action of the e-mini Dow Jones futures for the latter part of 2015 and into 2016. Declination of the Moon has been added in the lower panel of the chart. The correlation is not perfect, but it is consistent enough to warrant using lunar declination as a tool to help identify short term market swings, especially with an hourly or a 30 minute chart.

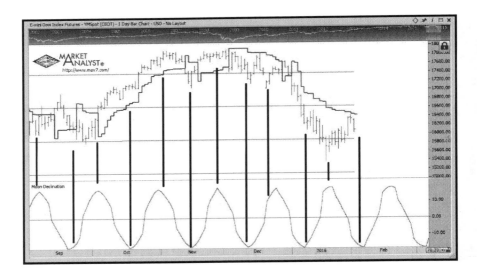

Figure 37 – Dow Jones and Moon Declination

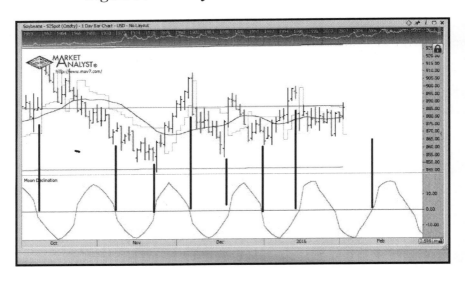

Figure 38 – Soybeans and Moon Declination

Figure 38 illustrates price action of Soybeans with lunar declination added in the lower pane of the chart. For a trader using 30 minute or hourly charts, the day when the Moon is at 0 degrees declination could prove to be an important time to initiate a trade on Soybeans.

10

CYCLES OF TIME

As discussed in the previous two chapters, Mercury and Venus travel around the Sun in quick fashion – 88 days and 225 days respectively. Table 4 presents the orbital times for the other planets.

Planet	Orbital Period Around Sun
Mercury	88 days
Venus	225 days
Earth	365 days
Mars	687 days
Jupiter	11.85 years
Saturn	29.42 years
Uranus	83.75 years
Neptune	163.74 years
Pluto	245.33 years

Table 4 – Orbital Periods of Planets

A synodic cycle is that length of time for a celestial body to complete an entire pattern as referenced from the fixed observation point of the Earth (geocentric). Such a pattern is usually taken to mean the time from when a planet is conjunct (0 degrees) to Sun to when it is again conjunct to the Sun. Such a pattern could also be the time from when a planet is conjunct (0 degrees) another planet to when it is again conjunct that planet. Table 5 presents various planet to planet synodic cycles.

	Earth	Mercury	Venus	Mars	Jupiter	Saturn	Uranus	Neptune	Pluto
Mercury	116 days		144.5 days	100.9 days	89.8 days	88.7 days	88.2 days	88.1 days	88.0 days
Venus	584 days	144.5 days		334.5 days	237.3 days	229.8 days	226.6 days	225.8 days	225.5 days
Mars	780 days	100.9 days	334.5 days		2.23 years	2.0 years	1.92 years	1.90 years	1.90 years
Jupiter	399 days	89.8 days	237.3 days	2.23 years		19.85 years	13.81 years	12.77 years	12.45 years
Saturn	376 days	88.7 days	229.8 days	2.0 years	19.85 years		45.26 years	35.68 years	33.40 years
Uranus	370 days	88.2 days	226.6 days	1.92 years	13.81 years	45.26 years		171.42 years	127.15 years
Neptune	367 days	88.1 days	225.8 days	1.90 years	12.77 years	35.68 years	171.42 years		492.34 years
Pluto	367 days	88.0 days	225.5 days	1.90 years	12.45 years	33.40 years	127.15 years	492.34 years	

Table 5 – Synodic Periods of Planets

As Table 5 shows, Saturn and Jupiter have a 19.85 year synodic period. In round figures, Saturn and Jupiter have a 20 year synodic period. This 20 year period is what W.D. Gann referred to as the Master Cycle.

Investors should focus on the 0, 90 and 180 degree aspects of this Master Cycle. Consider the following analysis of a Master Cycle:

Saturn was 0 degrees separated from Jupiter for the first 8 months of 1961. During 1961, the Dow Jones Industrial Average peaked at near 734 before declining to the 580 level for a drop of about 20 %.

In 1970 and into early 1971, Saturn and Jupiter came into a 180 degree aspect on a number of occasions. During this time frame the Dow Jones Industrial Average registered a significant low after making a 285 point drop (28 %) from a high in 1968.

From late-1975 to mid-1976 Saturn and Jupiter came into a 90 degree aspect on several occasions and the Dow Jones Industrial Average rallied hard and fast from a significant low made late in 1974.

In the first half of 1981, Saturn and Jupiter completed the Master Cycle and again were at a 0 degree aspect. This time frame marked a peak in the Dow Jones Industrial Average. Interestingly enough, following this peak, a sell-off of some 24% took place which cleared the decks for the start of a major bull market run.

The current Master Cycle that is unfolding started in 2000. From May to September 2000, Saturn and Jupiter were at a 0 degree aspect. This aspect marked the Dow Jones Industrial Average reaching a major high. In the first part of 2006 Saturn and Jupiter were at a 90 degree aspect and markets had an 8 percent decline before resuming an uptrend. From late 2010 through May 2011, Saturn and Jupiter were at a 180 degree aspect. During this period the market rallied smartly only to peak and fade in May just as this aspect was concluding. Saturn and Jupiter are scheduled to make a 90 degree aspect again from mid-2015 to the end of 2015 which will mark the ¾ interval of the Master Cycle. From December 2015 through early 2016, a significant sell-off on the Dow Jones Index occurred. While this came as a shock to many, it was simply a major interval of the overall Master Cycle manifesting itself.

Synodic Cycle or Planetary Advancement	Time
Saturn-Uranus cycle	45.26 years
½ of a Saturn-Uranus cycle	22.63 years
¼ of a Saturn-Uranus cycle	11.31 years
Jupiter-Saturn cycle	19.85 years
½ of a Jupiter-Saturn cycle	9.92 years
Jupiter-Uranus cycle	13.81 years
½ of a Jupiter-Uranus cycle	6.9 years
Jupiter-Neptune cycle	12.77 years
½ of a Jupiter-Neptune cycle	6.38 years
120 degree move of Saturn	9.8 years
60 degree move of Saturn	4.9 years
30 degree move of Uranus	6.97 years
Mars-Saturn cycle	2.0 years

Table 6 – Other Cyclic Intervals

Table 6 presents a number of other cyclical timeframes that one can use in assessing longer term behavior of stocks, commodities and indices.

As an example, consider that the Dow Jones Industrial Average registered a significant peak in 1929 and a significant low in 1974. This could well be a 45.26 year Saturn-Uranus synodic period in action. Consider also that in 2000 the markets registered a significant high and then a significant low in early 2009. Is this one-half of a Jupiter-Saturn Master Cycle? Markets registered a low in late 2002 and a significant low again in early 2009. Is this one-half of a Jupiter-Uranus 13.81 year synodic period?

11

THE MCWHIRTER METHOD

The McWhirter Method is the brainchild of astrologer Louise McWhirter who was active in New York in the 1930s.

Very little is known about Louise McWhirter, except that in 1937 she wrote the book *McWhirter Theory of Stock Market Forecasting*.

In my travels to places as far away as the British Library in London, England to research the subject of financial astrology, not once did I come across any other books by her. Not once did I find any other book from her era that even mentioned her name. All of this I find to be deeply mysterious.

There are three components to the McWhirter Method:

- The North Node movement in the zodiac

- The New Moon and the Dow Jones Industrial Average

- Planetary aspects to key natal planetary positions

The North Node and the Business Cycle

McWhirter closely followed the economic forecasts of Colonel Leonard P. Ayers at the Cleveland Trust Company. Colonel Ayers was a devout student of the stock market and was revered by the American government for his correlations between business activity and stock market indices. One of his more famous correlations related the number of operating blast furnaces in the American steel industry to stock market tops and bottoms.

It seems Ayers may also have been a student of astrology. Ayers and McWhirter observed a correlation between American economic activity and astrology. This correlation shows that the North Node of the Moon moving through the various signs of the zodiac aligns to periods of strength and weakness in economic activity. A full journey of the North Node around the twelve signs of the zodiac comprises one complete business cycle in the economy. In today's age of globalization and Central Bank co-ordinations, the business cycle can be viewed on a global scale.

So, what exactly is the North Node of the Moon?

As noted in Chapter 7, the Earth and the other planets orbit around the Sun in a plane of motion called the ecliptic plane. The Moon meanwhile orbits the Earth in a plane of motion called the lunar plane. Mathematically, two planes that are not parallel must intersect each other. The points of intersection are called the North Node and the South Node.

The mathematical concept of the Nodes was first recognized thousands of years ago by ancient Hindu astrologers who called the North Node *rahu* and the South Node *ketu*. In any horoscope chart, the North and South Nodes are 180 degrees opposite one another. Therefore, it is only necessary to study the position of one of the Nodes. McWhirter and Ayers focused only on the North Node. Modern astrologers today also focus mainly on the North Node.

The North Node is deemed to have dampening, suppressive forces similar to that of Saturn. So, at the peak of a business cycle, these dampening forces are at a minimum and at the low point in a business cycle these dampening forces are at their strongest.

The diagram in Figure 39 illustrates the intersection of the ecliptic and lunar planes.

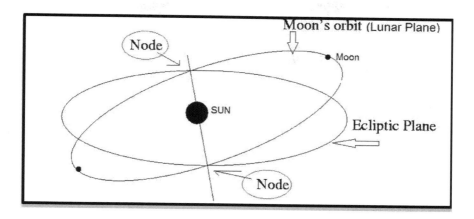

Figure 39 – The Lunar Nodes

Mathematically, to an observer positioned on Earth, it appears as though the Nodes are progressing backwards in a retrograde motion through the zodiac wheel. The length of time for the Nodes to pass through the twelve zodiac signs is 18.6 years. This means that every 1.55 years, the Nodes will enter into a different zodiac sign.

Using economic data from Colonel Ayers at the Cleveland Trust Company, McWhirter was able to discern the following:

- As the Node enters Aquarius, the low point of economic activity has been reached.

- As the Node leaves Aquarius and begins to transit through Capricorn and Sagittarius, the economy starts its return to more normal levels of activity.

- As the Node passes through Scorpio and Libra, the economy is functioning at above normal.

- As the Node transits through Leo, the high point in economic activity has been reached.

- As the Node transits through Cancer and Gemini, the economy is easing back towards normal.

- As the Node enters the sign of Taurus, the economy begins to slow.
- As the Node enters Aquarius, the low point of economic activity has been reached and a full 18.6 year cycle has been completed.

McWhirter further observed some secondary factors that can influence the tenor of economic activity in a good way, regardless of which sign the Node is in at the time:

- Jupiter being 0 degrees conjunct to the Node
- Jupiter being in Gemini or Cancer
- Pluto being at a favorable (30, 60 or 120 degree) aspect to the Node.

McWhirter also observed some secondary factors that can influence the tenor of economic activity in a bad way, no matter which sign the Node is in at the time:

- Saturn being 0, 90 or 180 degrees to the Node
- Saturn in Gemini or Cancer
- Uranus in Gemini
- Uranus being 0, 90 or 180 degrees to the Node
- Pluto being at an unfavorable (0, 90 or 180 degree) aspect to the Node.

To further illustrate the correlation between the Node and the business cycle, consider the following examples of when the Node was passing through Aquarius:

Immediately prior to 1859, the American economy had come under duress with the failure of the Ohio Life Insurance and Trust Company. In addition, bankers on Wall Street had overextended themselves with massive lending to railway companies seeking to profit from the masses of settlers heading west. In early 1859, the Node moved into Aquarius which signalled the low point in an economic cycle. The Node was 90 degrees square Uranus as well which meant the tenor of the cycle was further negatively influenced.

Economic slowdowns can irritate and polarize people. In London, Karl Marx penned *A Contribution to the Critique of Political Economy* (the precursor to *Das Kapital*) in early 1859. In America, the issue of slavery was being hotly debated. No sooner had the Node transited out of Aquarius, than the Civil War began in the United States.

In April 1896, the Node transited into Aquarius and the American economy (along with commodity prices) slumped when investors thought the Gold Standard would be abolished.

In mid-July 1914, the Node was in the latter stages of Pisces, on its way towards Aquarius and a low point in the economic cycle, when World War I broke out.

In mid-1933, the Node was about to enter into Aquarius thus signalling a low point in the economic cycle. This time period marked the depths of the Great Depression.

In early 1952, the Node was about to enter the sign of Aquarius as America found itself engaged in war in Korea.

In late 1970, the Node was again poised to enter Aquarius. America was deeply embroiled in the Vietnam War. War was also raging on the Indian sub-continent. Inflation was posing a problem to the global economy. Energy prices were crimping the North American economy. Tensions were rising between Arabs and Israelis in the Middle East.

In May 1989, the Node was again ready to enter Aquarius. Inflation was hurting the economy. In America, the Savings and Loans crisis was reaching a crescendo. Economic growth was low and tensions were again rising in the Middle East. Coalition forces would soon become engaged in Operation Desert Storm in response to Iraq's invasion of its neighbor, Kuwait.

In early 2008, the Node was again on the doorstep of the sign of Aquarius. As it entered Aquarius, it made a 0 degree aspect to Uranus. The completion of this particular 18.6 year economic cycle would be a harsh one with the entire capitalist system coming under extreme duress.

The Moon and the New York Stock Exchange

The second component of the McWhirter method pertains to the New York Stock Exchange which was founded in May 1792. There are several key features in the 1792 horoscope chart for the New York Stock Exchange.

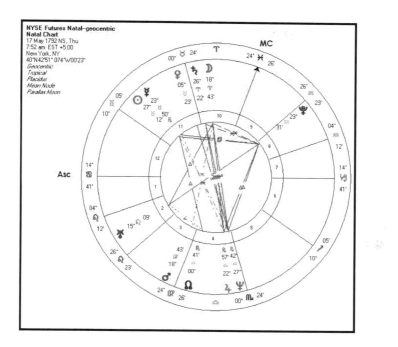

Figure 40 – Natal Birth Chart of the NYSE

The McWhirter method focuses on the Moon and its 29.5 day lunar cycle relative to these key features. Note in Figure 40 the position of the Ascendant and the Mid-Heaven. The Ascendant point (Asc) is at 14 degrees Cancer and the Mid-Heaven point (MC) is at 24 degrees Pisces. The 10th House itself spans the sign of Aries and a bit of the sign of Pisces. The ruling planet of Aries is Mars while the ruling planet of Pisces is Neptune. Thus, astrologers say that the NYSE is ruled by Mars and Neptune.

By studying the planetary positions in the zodiac wheel at the time of a New Moon, one can get a general sense of what the coming 29.5 day lunar cycle may have in store for the NYSE. Hard 0 or 90 degree aspects of the New Moon to ruling planets Mars and Neptune indicate a highly volatile lunar cycle to come. A lack of hard aspects usually means the current prevailing market trend will continue.

93

As the 29 day lunar cycle progresses, the McWhirter method demands that one be alert to times when the Moon makes 0 degree aspects to the natal Ascendant point (14 Cancer), the natal Mid-Heaven point (24 Pisces) and also Mars and Neptune. These aspects are times of strong probability for a short term trend change (inflection point) on the New York Stock Exchange.

At the time McWhirter was publishing her work, the Dow Jones Average was the main index used to quantify price action on the New York Stock Exchange. Today, there are many different indices used to track activity on the New York Exchange – the S&P 500 being a main one. However, the Dow Jones Average continues to be a widely followed index. In keeping with McWhirter's work, I use the Dow Jones Average when applying her technique to an US equity index. All too often I find that other global equity indices take their marching orders from what happens in New York.

The psychological theory behind this component of the McWhirter method is that the Moon has a strong effect on human emotion. The scientific basis for the Moon triggering emotional responses at these key locations remains a mystery of the entire McWhirter method. Hopefully in years to come scientists and psychologists who are exploring the field of cosmo-biology will propose some answers.

The Mysterious 14 Degrees of Cancer Point

So, why would the original founders of the New York Stock Exchange arrange it so that the Exchange commenced business on May 17 at a time when the Ascendant was at 14 degrees of Cancer? The answer may rest with the date the United States came into being. On July 4, 1776, the Sun was at 14 degrees of Cancer.

Rabbi Jonathan Cahn in his book *The Harbinger – The Ancient Mystery that Holds the Secret of America's Future*, notes that George Washington was officially sworn in as the first President of the United States of America on April 30, 1789 at 9:00 am in New York. At that hour, the transiting Moon was passing by 14 degrees of Cancer.

Many of the founding fathers of the United States were Freemasons. Reflecting on the notion that explorer Christopher Columbus may also have been associated with Masonic ideas, I looked further into his 1492 voyage that resulted in the discovery of the New World. In the early 1500s writer Bartolome de las Casas documented Columbus's story of when land was first sighted. As de las Casas notes, it was near mid-night on October 11, 1492 when a distant flickering light was spotted. At daybreak the next day, October 12, 1492, Columbus and his party went ashore to what is today the Bahamas. And with that, the New World had been discovered. Here is what in intriguing. The Moon on the evening of October 11, 1492 was passing by 14 degrees of Cancer in the zodiac. Is this a big part of the reason why America is fixated on 14 degrees of Cancer? Is this why the 14 degrees of Cancer position in the zodiac wheel figures prominently in the astrology of the New York Stock Exchange?

Consider the following example of McWhirter's lunar cycle technique for studying the Dow Jones Average. The New Moon in December 2015 occurred on the 10th day of December as the following horoscope wheel in Figure 41 depicts.

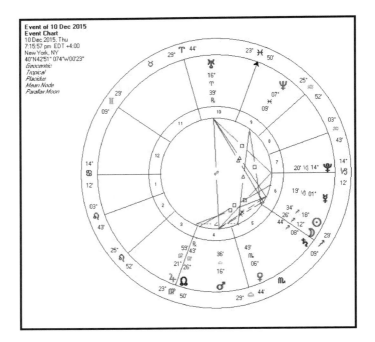

Figure 41 – New Moon of December 2015

Studying the movement of the Moon during December, 2015 shows that it will transit past Neptune and also 24 Pisces over the course of December 26-27. The Moon will also transit past 14 of Cancer on January 4, 2016.

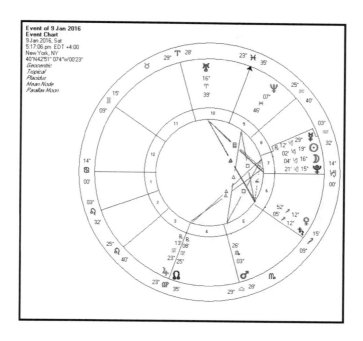

Figure 42 – New Moon of January 2016

The New Moon in January 2016 occurred on the 9th day as shown in Figure 42. Studying the movement of the Moon during January shows that it will transit past Neptune and also 24 Pisces within the span of January 12-14. The Moon will also transit past 14 of Cancer on January 22, 2016.

The chart in Figure 43 illustrates price action on the Dow Jones Average during the period encompassed by these New Moons. This chart has been overlaid with the key dates discussed above. Note how these critical dates align to inflection points on the Dow Jones Average.

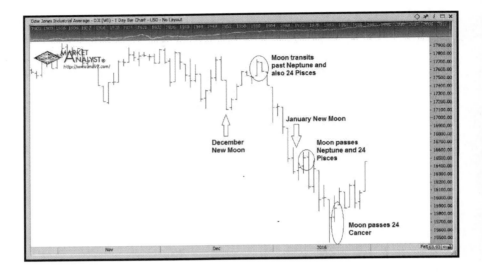

Figure 43 – Dow Jones and McWhirter Method

Individual Stocks and Commodities

The third part of the McWhirter method pertains to individual stocks and commodity futures. By studying the *First Trade horoscope* chart of a stock or commodity future, one can identify key planets and critical planetary aspects.

The First Trade horoscope is a horoscope wheel that depicts the positions of the planets on the date when the stock or commodity first started trading on a recognized exchange. By watching times when the transiting Sun and various transiting planets make aspects to these First Trade key positions, one can identify times during a calendar year when there will be a strong likelihood for a trend change.

This approach is based on transiting Sun and the major planets making aspects to the natal Sun, the natal Moon, natal Mars and natal Jupiter in the First Trade horoscope chart. All in all quite a complex approach. Therefore, when using the McWhirter method to study individual stocks or commodity futures, I prefer to simplify matters by being alert to those times when the following aspect events happen:

- Sun makes 0, 90, 180 degree aspects to natal Sun

- Sun makes 0 degree aspects to natal Jupiter

- Mars makes 0, 90, 180 degree aspects to natal Sun

- Mars makes 0 degree aspects to natal Mars

- Mars makes 0 degree aspects to natal Jupiter

- Transiting Saturn makes 0 and 90 degree aspects to natal Sun

- Transiting Jupiter makes 0 and 90 degree aspects to natal Sun.

I remain particularly alert to the 0 degree events. The 90 degree events are important and the 180 degree events less important. These aspect events are not necessarily frequent. Earth takes 365 days to orbit the Sun. Therefore, from our vantage point here on Earth we will see Sun making 0, 90 and 180 degree aspects to natal Sun only four times a year.

Mars takes 687 days to orbit the Sun. From our vantage point here on Earth we might see Mars make various aspects to natal Sun, natal Mars and natal Jupiter only a handful of times each year.

Saturn takes 29.42 years to orbit the Sun and Jupiter 11.85 years. From our vantage point here on Earth, Saturn and Jupiter will make aspects to the natal Sun very infrequently. But, when these aspects do occur, they can be powerful events.

Not every stock or commodity will exhibit alignments to all of these various aspects. When examining a stock or commodity future, it is advised to look back in time several years to see which aspects most often repeat themselves. This will then give you a valid model to follow going forward.

McWhirter Rules for Aspect Angles

- In the case of a 0 degree conjunction or 180 degree opposition, it is acceptable to have planets within 10 degrees of each other.

- In the case of a 90 degree square, it is acceptable to have planets within 5 degrees of each other.

Consider the following examples of the McWhirter method applied to Soybeans, 30 Year Bonds and an individual stock, E-Commerce giant Alibaba.

Soybeans

Soybean futures started trading in Chicago on October 5, 1936. The horoscope in Figure 44 illustrates the planetary placements at that time. Sun is at 12 degrees Libra. Jupiter is at 18 degrees Sagittarius.

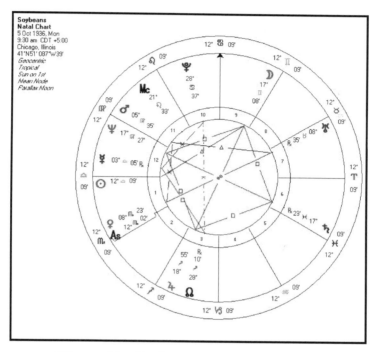

Figure 44 – Soybeans Natal Horoscope

The price chart in Figure 45 illustrates Soybeans price action from mid-2014 through early 2016. This chart has been overlaid with events of Sun transiting past natal Sun and also Sun transiting past natal Jupiter.

Note at the far left of the chart that in October 2014 a significant trend change occurred as Sun passed by the natal Sun location. This price rally eventually faded, but received more energy as Sun passed

101

by the natal Jupiter position in early December 2014. In October 2015, as Sun passed by the natal Sun location quite the opposite occurred. The trend took a negative turn and price declined to levels not seen since 2008. A subsequent rally attempt was stalled in its tracks as transiting Sun passed by the natal Jupiter location.

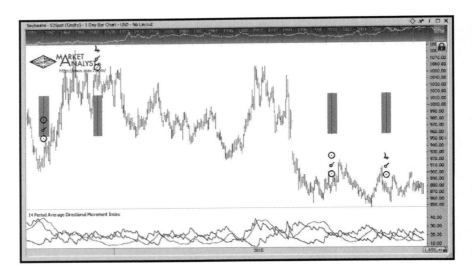

Figure 45 – Soybeans and the McWhirter Method

The transiting Moon can also be used as a tool to analyse the Soybean market, much like the Moon is used in analysing the NYSE and Dow Jones Average. In Figure 44 note that the Mid-Heaven location in the Soybeans natal chart is at 12 Cancer and the Ascendant is at 12 Libra. Within a 29.5 day lunar cycle, the Moon will pass each of these critical locations once.

The price chart in Figure 46 illustrates the times when Moon passed the Soybean Mid-Heaven and Ascendant during November 2015 through early January 2016. Some flexibility must be afforded to this method due to week-ends when there is no trading on Soybean futures. In such cases, price responses can reasonably be expected to occur on the Friday ahead of the week-end or on the Monday following.

For a trader following the Soybean market, these Moon aspects will be best seen to align to price swings using an hourly or 30 minute chart.

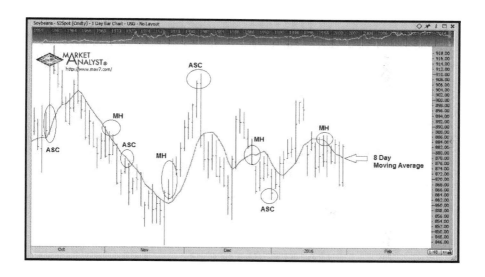

Figure 46 – Soybeans and Transiting Moon

30 Year Bonds

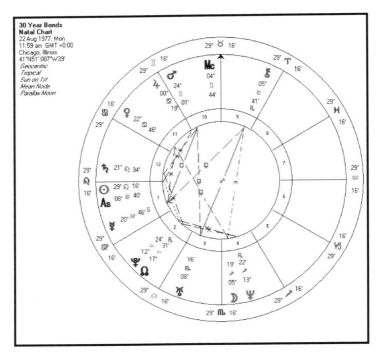

Figure 47 – 30 Year Bond Futures Natal Horoscope

30 Year Bond futures started trading on a recognized exchange on August 22, 1977. The horoscope wheel in Figure 47 illustrates the planetary placements at that time.

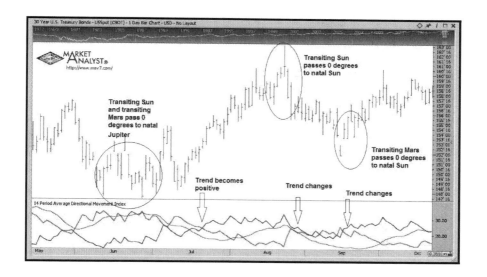

Figure 48– 30 Year Bonds and the McWhirter Method

The chart in Figure 48 illustrates price action of these Bond futures from May through October, 2015. The chart has been overlaid with several astrology events - Sun passing the natal Jupiter location, Mars passing the natal Jupiter location, Sun passing the natal Sun position and Mars passing the natal Sun position. Sun and Mars passing the natal Jupiter location resulted in a price low and the end of a three month decline in price. Sun passing natal Sun in August resulted in a price high and a trend change. Mars passing the natal Sun location in September created another trend change.

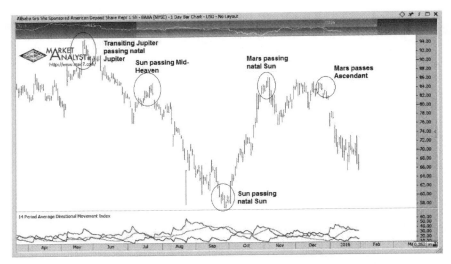

Figure 49 – Alibaba (BABA) and the McWhirter Method

E-Commerce giant Alibaba started trading on the NYSE on September 19, 2014. Alibaba can best be thought of as the Chinese equivalent to Amazon. The chart in Figure 49 illustrates Alibaba's price action from April 2015 to early 2016.

This chart has been overlaid with several key astrological events as per the McWhirter method. Note how these events align to price inflection points. Using a suitable technical indicator to measure trend, one could have taken full and fair advantage of these price swings.

If you are seeking lists of stock First Trade dates, my website www.investingsuccess.ca has links to tables of First Trade dates for numerous stocks In my annual Financial Astrology Almanacs, I cover a wide range of commodity futures contracts and the annual astrological events that stand to create price trend changes.

The following pages contain the First Trade horoscopes for several commodity futures contracts.

Gold

On the 12th of September 1919, the Bank of England made arrangements with N.M. Rothschild & Sons for the formation of a free gold market in which there would be an official price for gold quoted each day. At 11:00 am on September 12, 1919, the first Gold price fixing took place, with the five principal gold bullion traders and refiners of the era participating. These traders and refiners were N.M. Rothschild & Sons, Mocatta & Goldsmid, Pixley & Abell, Samuel Montagu & Co. and Sharps Wilkins.

Many significant price highs and lows on Gold have shown an astrological relation to the planetary positions in the Gold Fix horoscope shown in Figure 50.

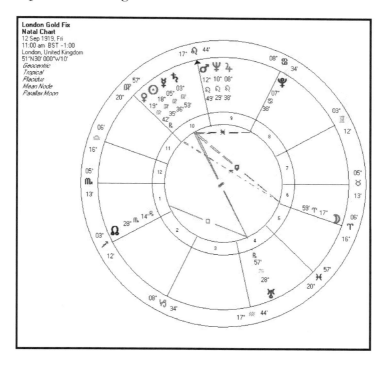

Figure 50 - London Gold Fix Horoscope

Gold prices continued to be set using the daily London Gold fix for many years until the advent of the Gold futures contract in America.

Gold futures started trading on the New York Mercantile Exchange on December 31, 1974. Figure 51 illustrates the First Trade horoscope.

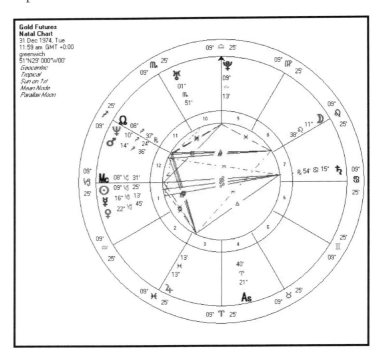

Figure 51 – Gold Futures First Trade Horoscope

Note how Mars and Neptune are conjunct to each other in the 1919 Gold Fix horoscope and also conjunct one another in the 1974 Futures horoscope. In the Gold futures horoscope, Moon is at 11 degrees of Leo. In the 1919 Gold Fix horoscope, Mars and Neptune are within a couple degrees of this 11 of Leo point. All very curious indeed. If you are following Gold prices, pay attention to times when Sun and Venus are conjunct each other as in the 1919 horoscope. Note times when Sun and Mars pass conjunct to the 8 to 12 degree part of Leo, where Jupiter, Neptune and Mars are located in the 1919 horoscope. Pay attention to those times when Sun and Mars pass conjunct to the Sun's location in the 1974 Gold futures horoscope. Lastly, for a long term study, note the times when Saturn and Uranus are 0, 90 and 180 degrees apart. In the 1919 Gold Fix horoscope, these two heavy-weights were 180 degrees apart.

Silver

Silver futures started trading on a recognized financial exchange in 1933. Figure 52 illustrates the planetary placements at the date.

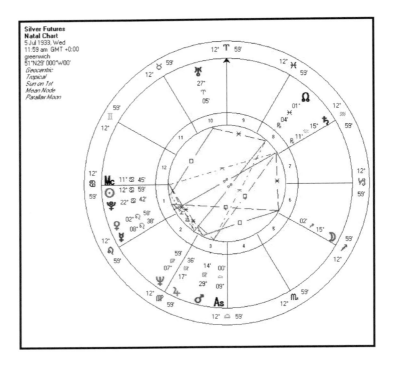

Figure 52 – Silver Futures First Trade Horoscope

Sun passing 0 degrees to natal Sun and also Mars passing 0 degrees to natal Sun are times to watch carefully if following the Silver market.

Copper

The First Trade Date for Copper futures was July 29, 1988. Figure 53 illustrates the planetary placements at that date.

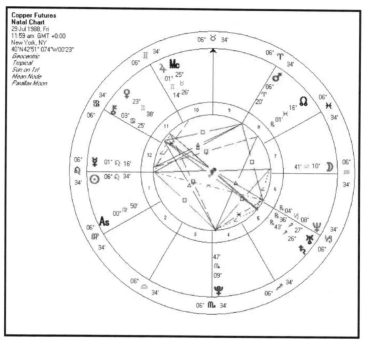

Figure 53 – Copper Futures First Trade Horoscope

In this horoscope, note that Sun and Mercury are within five degrees of each other. If following the Copper market, be alert at times when Mercury makes 0 and 180 degree aspects to the Sun. Watch also times when Mercury is Retrograde.

Canadian Dollar, British Pound, Japanese Yen

These three futures instruments all started trading on May 16th, 1972 at the Chicago Mercantile Exchange. Figure 54 illustrates the planetary placements at that time.

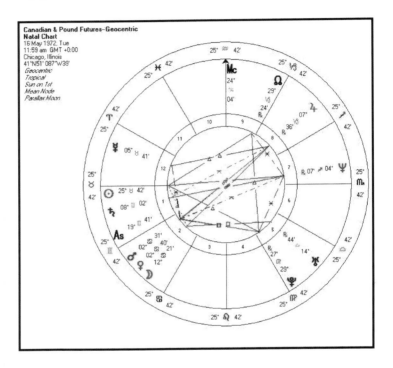

Figure 54 – Canadian Dollar, British Pound, Japanese Yen

In this horoscope, note that Mars is conjunct Venus. Watch for such conjunctions to occur if following these currencies. Watch also for times when Sun passes conjunct to natal Mars and natal Jupiter.

EuroCurrency

The Euro became the official currency for the European Union on January 1, 2002 when Euro bank notes became freely and widely circulated. Arguably there may be another date – January 1999 when the E.U. zone nations were required to establish a fixed rate of exchange between their currencies and the Euro currency. But, I prefer the 2002 date because of the peculiar relation between Venus and Sun. A look at the geocentric natal First Trade chart for this date in Figure 55 reveals Sun and Venus are very near to Superior Conjunction. In fact, the exact date of Superior Conjunction was January 14, 2002.

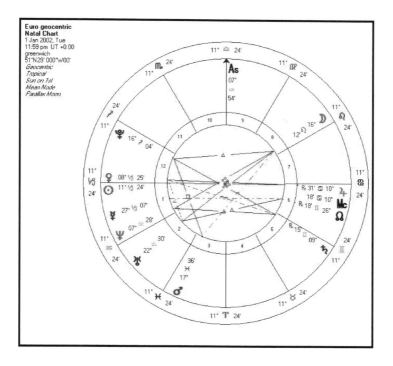

Figure 55 – Eurocurrency Natal Horoscope

If following the Eurocurrency, be alert to Sun passing conjunct to natal Sun and for Venus Superior and Inferior conjunctions.

113

Australian Dollar

Australian dollar futures started trading on the Chicago Mercantile Exchange on January 13, 1987. As the horoscope in Figure 56 shows, Sun and Mercury are at a Superior Conjunction at 22-23 degrees Capricorn. Watch for these conjunctions of following the Australian Dollar. Sun passing 0 degrees conjunct to natal Sun events should also be noted.

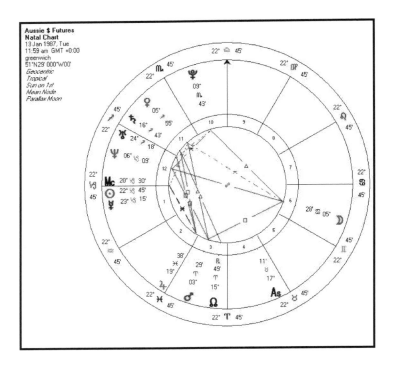

Figure 56 – Australian Dollar Futures First Trade Horoscope

10 Year Treasury Notes

10 Year Treasury Notes started trading in Chicago on May 3, 1982. Figure 57 illustrates the planetary placements at that time.

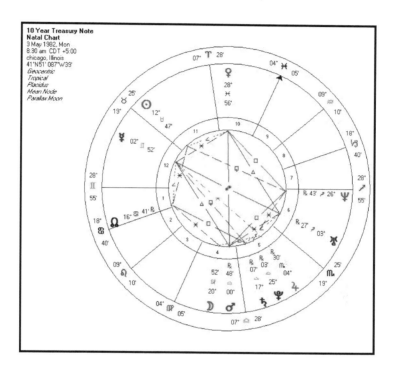

Figure 57 – 10 Year Treasury Notes Natal Horoscope

If following 10 Year Treasuries, be alert to Mars passing 0 degrees conjunct to natal Sun, natal Venus and natal Mercury. These are times when you may well experience price inflection points.

Wheat, Corn, Oats

Wheat, Corn and Oats futures all share the same first trade date of January 2, 1877. The horoscope in Figure 58 shows planetary placements at this date.

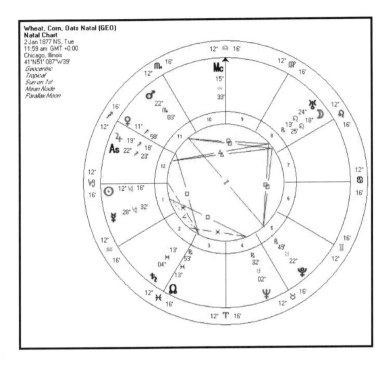

Figure 58 - Wheat, Corn, Oats First Trade Horoscope

If trading these commodities, be alert to conjunction events of Sun/natal Sun and Mars natal Sun. I have also noted price responses to Mars and Venus declination maxima and minima events. Mercury Retrograde events are important as well.

Soybeans

Soybean futures started trading in Chicago on October 5, 1936. The horoscope in Figure 59 illustrates the planetary placements at that time. The location of the Sun is intriguing. Notice how it is exactly 90 degrees to the location of the Sun in the First Trade chart for Wheat, Corn and Oats? Is it possible the regulatory officials who determine these First Trade dates know more about Astrology than we may think?

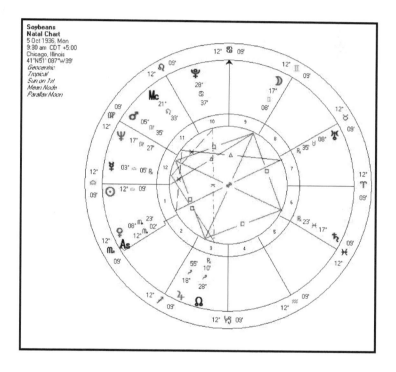

Figure 59 – Soybean Futures First Trade Horoscope

If trading Soybeans, be alert to conjunction events of Sun/natal Sun and Mars natal Sun. I have also noted price responses to Mars and Venus declination maxima and minima events. Mercury Retrograde events are important as well.

Crude Oil

West Texas Intermediate Crude Oil futures started trading on a recognized exchange for the first time on March 30, 1983. A unique alignment of celestial points can be seen in the horoscope in Figure 60. Notice how Mars, North Node, (Saturn/Pluto/Moon) and Neptune conspire to form a rectangle.

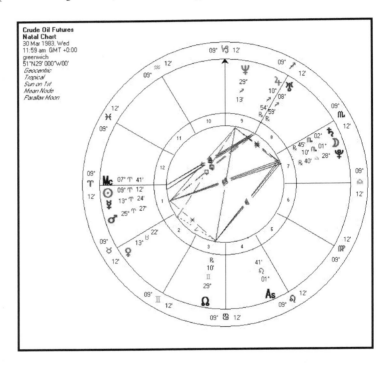

Figure 60 – Crude Oil Futures Natal Horoscope

Sun and Mars passing 0 degrees conjunct to the corners of this rectangle often align to price inflection points on Crude Oil. However, note that Crude Oil futures can be extremely volatile and therefore difficult to trade.

Cotton

After much painstaking research sifting through back-editions of New York newspapers, I have come to conclude that Cotton futures first started trading on June 20, 1870. The horoscope wheel in Figure 61 illustrates planetary placements at that time.

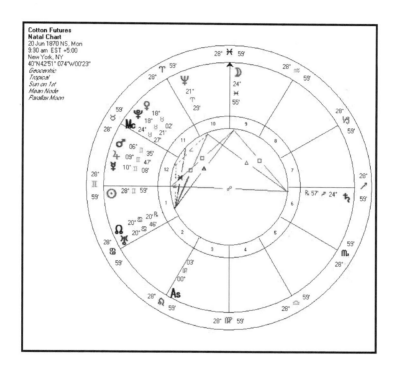

Figure 61 – Cotton Futures First Trade Horoscope

If following the Cotton market, be alert to Sun passing 0 degrees conjunct to natal Sun and for events where Venus passes 0 degrees to natal Moon. Note that the natal Moon is curiously situated at 24 Pisces – the same location as the Mid-Heaven of the New York Stock Exchange. Such are the curiosities of financial astrology.

119

Coffee

Coffee futures started trading in New York in early March of 1882. The horoscope wheel in Figure 62 illustrates planetary placements at that time.

In the Coffee horoscope, note the 180 degree aspect between Sun and Uranus. The McWhirter methodology cautions that it is not wise to invest in situations where this sort of aspect exists because one will experience many wild ups and downs in price over time. A quick look at a 10 year price chart of Coffee reveals a price range characterized by many wild swings.

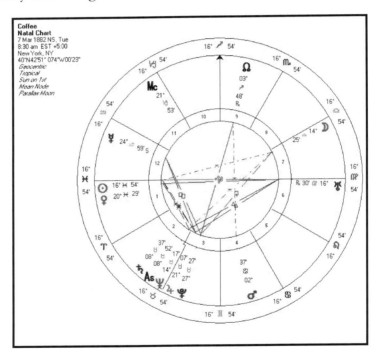

Figure 62 – Coffee Futures First Trade Horoscope

Note also that Sun is 180 degrees to Uranus in this horoscope and Sun is practically conjunct Venus.

Sugar

For some time I was of the opinion that Sugar had started trading in New York in early January of 1881. However, recent data from the archives of 1930s astrologer Evangeline Adams suggests that Sugar started trading on August 17, 1887.

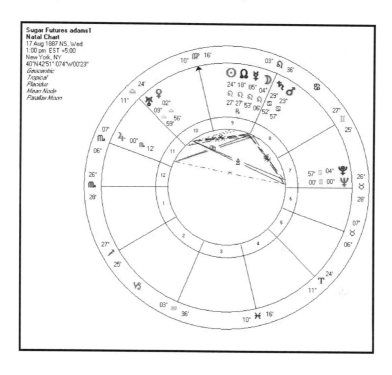

Figure 63 – Sugar Futures Natal Horoscope

Cocoa

Cocoa futures started trading in New York on October 2, 1925. The horoscope wheel in Figure 64 illustrates planetary placements at that time.

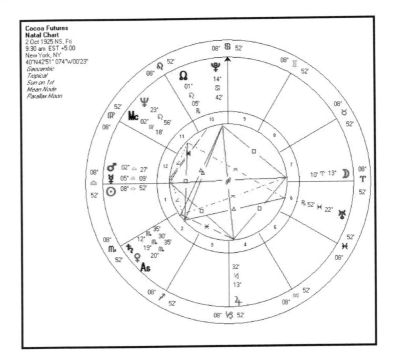

Figure 64 – Cocoa Futures First Trade Horoscope

Note that Sun and Mercury are conjunct. Pay close attention to Mercury at Superior and Inferior conjunction for price inflection points. Watch also the easterly and westerly elongation maximums of Mercury.

Lean Hogs

Lean Hogs futures started trading in Chicago on February 28 of 1966. The horoscope wheel in Figure 65 illustrates planetary placements at that time.

I have studied Lean Hogs in detail and the most repetitive astro event that I can find that aligns to trend changes is that of Mercury Retrograde.

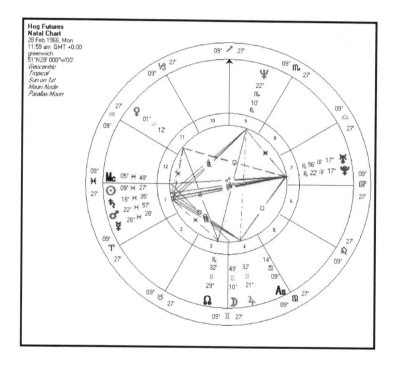

Figure 65 – Lean Hogs Futures Natal Horoscope

M.G. Bucholtz

12

THE TREND

The trend is your friend. Practically all investors have heard this expression before. Yet, so many choose to ignore it. I make it very clear to all who subscribe to my *Astrology E-Alert* newsletter that they should at all times be aware of the prevailing price trend whether they are trading a commodity futures contract, an individual stock or just assessing a market index. I mentioned the importance of trend in the opening part of this book. And, now to drive the point home one last time, I am including this brief chapter on the subject.

If there is one thing you simply must take away from this book, let it be the notion that if the trend changes at a significant astrological event, that trend change is to be taken *seriously*. In other words, there is no magic or trickery to financial astrology. People routinely ask me where I see the price of Gold in 6 months or where I see the S&P 500 going over the next year. My answer to all such questions remains steadfast – I don't know. Watch the trend and if it changes at an astrological event, then take action, I tell them. Stay with the trend until it changes at the next astrological event, I further remind them. Think of these trend changes if you will as changes in human emotion, I say.

At the outset of this book, I stated that I believed that solar wind affecting our bodily electromagnetic circuitry was responsible for changes in emotion. While I continue to feel this is true, I will leave you with another idea that I find myself grappling with. I struggle with the idea that some of the major players on the global markets often seek to orchestrate and dare I say manipulate the markets. The average investor is certainly not well-schooled on astrological events. Nor is the average investor well-rehearsed on the notion of trend.

The media scoffs at astrology all while focusing on abstract analyst price forecasts. This then leaves the playing field wide open for sophisticated players to induce trend changes at astrological events. As these players manipulate the markets at key astrological events, human emotion then kicks into gear and the investing masses either enter the market or leave the market in a herd-like mentality. This mentality is aided by our bodily electromagnetic circuitry being impacted by solar wind particles and further fueled by the media.

But, back to the subject of trend.

If there is a guru on the subject of trend, then his name is probably J. Welles Wilder. Mr. Wilder is an engineer by educational training, but spent much of his career actively trading the financial markets. Along the way he used his engineering prowess to develop mathematical indicators that measure trend.

One of his earliest developments was the Directional Movement Indicator, or DMI as it is often called. Wilder's DMI looks at the daily price movements. If price today closes above yesterday's price, the incremental difference is called +DM. If price today closes below yesterday's price, the incremental difference is called –DM. Wilder then expresses the +DM or –DM as a fraction of True Range. The True Range of a price is the largest of either (1) today's high and today's low (2) today's high and yesterday's close (3) today's low and yesterday's close. These various +/- DM fractions of True Range are called +DI and –DI.

To make the whole thing usable, Wilder then sums up all of the +DI numbers and all of the –DI numbers over the past trailing 14 days. He plots the +DI values and the –DI values. If the +DI plot line is above the –DI plot line, Wilder says the trend is positive. If the –DI plot line is above the +DI plot line, Wilder says the trend is negative.

Consider the following chart of the Nasdaq 100 Index. On the bottom panel of this chart one can see the DMI indicator plot. In this example, the trend is clearly negative. The proper way to view this indicator is in color on your computer screen. Most market data platforms will have the DMI indicator already built in. All you have to do is set the period to 14 days and then select the colors for the output lines.

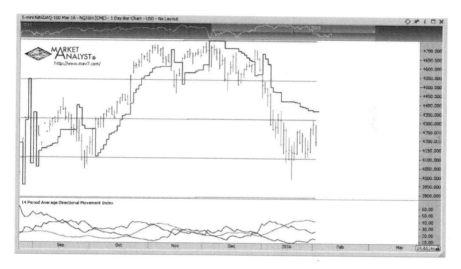

Figure 66 – Trend Indicators

Another of Wilder's inventions is the Wilder Volatility Index. In this method, Wilder calculates the True Ranges for each of the past seven trailing days and computes the Average True Range. He then multiples this Average True Range by a constant 'C' (something in the range of 2.5 to 3.0) to obtain Average True Range times Constant (ARC). The trend is deemed to have changed when price moves one ARC from the most favorable recent closing price.

The plot of the Nasdaq 100 in Figure 66 shows the Wilder Volatility Index overlaid on the price bars. The proper way to appreciate this Index is in color on your computer screen. Not all market data platforms will come equipped with this Volatility Index as a built-in function. Try to obtain a market data platform that does have the Volatility Index. You will have control over the period for the

Average True Range. I have found that a period n=6 works well. You will also have control over the constant 'C'. I normally start with C=3. I then examine the plot of the Volatility Index to see how quickly it has responded to recent swings in price. If necessary, I will adjust the value of 'C' to make the Volatility Index better fit recent trend changes.

With these two indicators, I then set about identifying the various astrological events discussed in this book. As they draw closer, I keep a close eye on the DMI and on the Volatility Index for evidence of a trend change. Once I see the trend change, then and only then do I contemplate an actionable trade.

13

FINAL THOUGHTS

This manuscript has taken you on an extensive journey through many facets of financial astrology from Inferior Conjunctions to Quantum Lines. Applying astrology to trading and investing is a skill that often takes time to develop. I encourage you to study as many price charts as you can. Identify the various astrological features and events discussed in this book. Take note of how and when the price trend changes at these events. I am certain that before long you will turn your back on the television commentators and the analysts sporting vague models of future earnings and expected prices and embrace financial astrology as your preferred method of making trading and investing decisions.

Welcome to the world of financial astrology. I hope that your experiences with astrology will be as gratifying as mine have been.

M.G. Bucholtz

14

GLOSSARY OF TERMS

Apogee (also called Aphelion): most commonly discussed in terms of the Earth and Moon. Because of the Moon's slightly elliptical pattern of rotation around the Earth, there will be times when it is far from Earth and there will be times when it is close to Earth. The time when the Moon is farthest from Earth is called *apogee*. Can also be applied to discussions concerning Mercury and the Sun.

Ascendant (Asc): One of four cardinal points on a horoscope, the Ascendant is situated in the East.

Aspect: The angular relationship between two planets measured in degrees.

Autumnal Equinox (also called Vernal Equinox): That time of the calendar year (around September 20) when Sun is at 0 degrees Libra.

Celestial Equator Plane: Earth is slightly tilted (approximately 23 degrees) relative to the ecliptic plane. Projecting the Earth's equator into space produces the celestial equator plane.

Conjunct: An angular relationship of 0 degrees between two planets.

Cosmo-biology: the science of how cosmic events affect human behavior.

Descendant (Dsc): One of four cardinal points on a horoscope, the Descendant is situated in the West.

Ecliptic Plane: the plane of motion that planets adhere to as they orbit the Sun.

Elongation: the angle between the planet and the Sun, using Earth as a reference point.

Ephemeris: A daily tabular compilation of planetary and lunar positions. Can be in either geocentric or heliocentric format.

Equinox: An event occurring twice annually, an equinox event marks the time when the tilt of the Earth's axis is neither toward or away from the Sun.

Fibonacci: properly known as Filius Bonacci, was a 13th century mathematician who is credited with reviving the notion of quadratic equations and sequences.

Fibonacci Sequence: numerical sequence 1,1,2,3,5,8,13 etc... where a number is the sum of the two prior numbers. Also called the Golden Sequence.

First Trade horoscope: A zodiac chart depicting the positions of the planets at the date a stock or a commodity future contract commenced trading on a recognized financial exchange.

First Trade date: The date a stock or commodity futures contract first began trading on a recognized exchange.

Full Moon: From a vantage point situated on Earth, when the Moon is seen to be 180 zodiac degrees to the Sun.

Gann Fan Lines: vector lines emanating from price highs or lows constructed using square root mathematics.

Gann Planetary Lines: lines on a price chart created by converting heliocentric planetary position into price by way of the Wheel of 24.

Geocentric Astrology: That version of astrology in which the vantage point for determining planetary aspects is the Earth.

Glyphs: symbols used to denote planets and zodiac signs.

Golden Mean: the unique mathematical solution to the quadratic equation $y^2 - y - 1 = 0$. Also known as phi.

Heliocentric Astrology: That version of astrology in which the vantage point for determining planetary aspects is the Sun.

Immum Coeli (IC): One of four cardinal points on a horoscope, the Immum Coeli is situated in the North.

Inferior Conjunction: with reference to Mercury or Venus, is that time when the heliocentric planet is 0 degrees to Earth.

Lunar Eclipse: A lunar eclipse occurs when the Sun, Earth, and Moon are aligned with the Earth in the middle. The Earth blocks the Sun's rays from striking the Moon.

Lunar Month: see Synodic Month

Lunar Orbit Plane: the plane of motion that the Moon follows in its orbit of Earth.

Mid-Heaven (MC): One of four cardinal points on a horoscope, the Mid-Heaven is situated in the South.

New Moon: From a vantage point situated on Earth, when the Moon is seen to be 0 degrees to the Sun.

North Node of Moon (also called Rahu): The intersection points between the Moon's plane and Earth's ecliptic are termed the North and South nodes. Astrologers tend to focus on the North node and Ephemeris tables clearly list the zodiacal position of the North Node for each calendar day.

Opposition: An angular relationship of 180 degrees between two planets.

Orb: The amount of flexibility or tolerance given to an aspect.

Perigee (also called Perihelion): most commonly discussed in terms of the Earth and Moon. Because of the Moon's slightly elliptical pattern of rotation around the Earth, there will be times when it is far from Earth and there will be times when it is close to Earth. The time when the Moon is closest from Earth is called *perigee*. Can also be applied to discussions concerning Mercury and the Sun.

Phi: see the Golden Mean

Retrograde motion: The apparent backwards motion of a planet through the zodiac signs when viewed from a vantage point on Earth.

Quantum Line: concept developed by author Fabio Oreste that posits price action will find support or resistance at levels defined by the general formula Nx360 +PSO.

Sidereal Month: The Moon orbits Earth with a slightly elliptical pattern in approximately 27.3 days, relative to an observer situated on a fixed frame of reference such as the Sun.

Sidereal Orbital Period: The time required for a planet to make one full orbit of the Sun as viewed from a fixed vantage point on the Sun.

Solar Eclipse: A solar eclipse occurs when the Moon passes between the Sun and Earth and fully or partially blocks the Sun.

Solar Fire Gold: software program sold by developer Astrolabe.

Solar Wind: energy emitted from the Sun into the vastness of space.

Solstice: An event occurring twice annually which marks the time when the Sun reaches its highest or lowest attitude above the horizon at noon.

Spiral Calendar: concept trademarked by Christopher Carolan in which cycles are identified based on the square root of a Fibonacci Sequence term multiplied by 29.5 days.

Spring Equinox: That time of the calendar year (around March 20) when Sun is at 0 degrees Aries.

Square of Nine: an array of numbers with starting point of 1. By moving clockwise and adding 1 unit, a square array can be constructed in which numbers in the array are related to one another by square root mathematics.

Superior Conjunction: with reference to Mercury or Venus, is when the heliocentric planet is 180 degrees to Earth

Synodic Month: During one sidereal month, Earth has revolved part way around the Sun, making the average apparent time between one New Moon and the next New Moon longer than the sidereal month at approximately 29.5 days. Also called a lunar month.

Synodic Orbital Period: The time required for a planet to make one full orbit of the Sun as viewed from a fixed vantage point on Earth.

Theory of Relativity: Einstein's theory that objects in space can distort time due to their mass.

Universal Clock: Jeanne Long's the patented version of Gann's Wheel of 24.

Universal Gravitation: Isaac Newton's theory that planets are attracted to one another by gravity.

VIX: a measure of S&P 500 volatility.

Wheel of 24: a wheel divided into 24 segments of 15 degrees each. The inner potion of the Wheel contains degree readings 1 through 360. The outer portion of the Wheel contains price data. The Wheel allows for easy conversion of planetary longitudinal position to price.

Zodiac: an imaginary encircling of the 360 degrees of the planetary system divided into twelve equal portions of 30 degrees each.

15

ABOUT THE AUTHOR

Malcolm Bucholtz, B.Sc, MBA is a graduate of Queen's University Faculty of Engineering in Canada. He received his MBA degree from Heriot Watt University in Scotland. After working in Canadian industry for far too many years, Malcolm followed his passion for the financial markets by becoming an Investment Advisor/Commodity Trading Advisor with an independent brokerage firm in western Canada. Today, he resides in western Canada where he trades the financial markets using technical chart analysis, esoteric mathematics and the astrological principles outlined in this book.

Malcolm maintains both a website (www.investingsuccess.ca) and a blog where he provides traders and investors with astrological insights into the financial markets. He also offers a monthly **Astrology E-Alert** service where subscribers receive bi-weekly previews of pending astrological events that stand to influence markets.

M.G. Bucholtz

16

INDEX

Market Analyst Software

Throughout this publication, I have made repeated reference to Market Analyst Software.

If you are curious about this software platform and would like to try it for a free evaluation period, simply load the following link into your browser.

http://www.mav8.com/investingsuccess